# CHRIST AND THE AMERICAS WORKBOOK

*and Study Guide*

—With Answer Key—

# CHRIST
# AND
# THE AMERICAS
# WORKBOOK

*and Study Guide*

—With Answer Key—

*By*

Belinda T. Mooney

*Based on the text by*

Anne W. Carroll

TAN Books
Gastonia, North Carolina

ISBN: 978-0-89555-744-5

Cover illustration credit: *Landing of Columbus*, by John Vanderlyn, used with permission of Architect of the Capitol, Washington, D.C.



Printed and bound in the United States of America.

TAN Books
Gastonia, North Carolina
TANBooks.com
2011

# Dedication

In Honor of the Most Holy Name
and in Adoration of the
Most Holy Face of Jesus Christ.

I Praise You, Lord,
I Bless Your Holy Name,
I Adore Your Holy Face.
I deeply desire to walk in the light of Your Face
all the days of my life.

—Belinda T. Mooney, 2000

## Acknowledgment

I want to thank my son Jarred for all the help he gave me in preparing the manuscripts for both of the workbooks that accompany Anne Carroll's texts. For *Christ the King, Lord of History—Workbook and Study Guide*, he assisted me in typing the chapters by hand, using a dictaphone at the age of 12. This typing was by far the hardest part of the work. For *Christ and the Americas—Workbook and Study Guide*, he assisted me with the editing of all the chapters, typing the corrections for me and pointing out errors. Also, I thank him for giving me the time to sit and do the work necessary for each chapter by caring for the younger children and keeping the house running when I was busy writing. Without Jarred's help, these two workbooks could not have been completed. I thank God for blessing me with such a wonderful son and for the gift of home schooling him and my other children.

# A Message to the Student

Welcome to this *Workbook* for *Christ and the Americas*. This *Workbook* was designed to help you make good use of Anne Carroll's textbook, *Christ and the Americas*, which is an excellent text for understanding the basics of U.S. and Central and South American history from a Catholic perspective.

If possible, it is preferable to have completed the other text, *Christ the King—Lord of History*, before moving on to *Christ and the Americas*. World history sets American history in proper perspective. Because so much of what you have read in world history will come into play now in American history, be sure to coordinate the time periods/chapters in *Christ and the Americas* with specific chapters of *Christ the King—Lord of History*. By taking just a moment to review the *Christ the King—Lord of History* chapters that correspond to chapters in *Christ and the Americas*, you will greatly refresh your memory and have a better set-up for these chapters.

Just like *Christ the King—Lord of History*, *Christ and the Americas* is not a text to simply read through and then expect yourself to remember. Without some sort of reinforcement, the material will simply become a blur in your mind. In order to remember the information and to see how the history of the world is intimately linked with that of the Catholic Church, you have to continue to work through the material and have it presented in different formats. I have created this *Workbook* for *Christ and the Americas* to help you go over the material. This *Workbook* covers almost every major topic from the text.

Whether you are an adult working independently to learn history or a student in a Catholic school or homeschool, I recommend that you use the *Workbook* as a guide before you go through each chapter, to assist yourself in focusing on the most important elements. Then answer the questions once you have finished reading the chapter. Later, you can use the *Workbook*, with the answers filled in, as a review. In that scenario, you are studying the material in-depth three times besides reading the chapter! You could also use the questions in the text at the end of each chapter as a test.

### Study Tips

When you read *Christ and the Americas*, take the initiative in learning and remembering the material! Take notes as you read through the text. Brief notes in the form of words, phrases and dates can be so useful and will not stop your progress in reading the chapter (the way copying a whole sentence would). For more complicated material, it is highly recommended that you make yourself timelines and charts to organize it for clearer understanding and better retention. Charts help to detail and group information in a way that is more understandable and more easily accessible.

Do not rush through the material. Read the chapter, complete the *Workbook* on that chapter, do selected projects and extra reading—completely mastering the material before moving on to the next chapter. Compose a short summary of the chapter (orally or in writing) to help you solidify the concepts. There are 26 chapters, which could be completed in 1 to 1½ weeks each, with longer time periods for larger chapters. Or, *Christ and the Americas* could be used for a two-year course, as recommended by Mrs. Carroll.

I highly recommend that you make two lists for yourself after finishing each chapter—one list called "Notes from this Chapter" and the other called "Questions/possible research areas from this Chapter." You could keep these lists in a notebook, or you could write them out in the blank space at the end of the chapters in this *Workbook*. These lists will help you to master the material in each chapter, to think it through and to "make it your own."

You will note that chapters 12, 17, 21 and 25 all relate to Latin American history and therefore go together. If it helps, you may want to read these in chronological order to make more sense of the sequence of history in Latin America. At the very least, review chapter 12 again before starting on 17.

## The Catholic Meaning of History

Remember, the more times you see the information in different forms, the better you will retain it and the more clearly you will understand history. Eventually you will feel as though you are on a road with a clear sense of your direction, knowing and understanding what is to the north, south, east and west. You will see clearly what happened before you in history and how that is affecting what is happening now. You will understand how we got to where we are today. You will see how God has worked through so many individuals and how people have affected history because of their cooperation or lack of cooperation with His Will.

Especially in *Christ and the Americas*, you will see how the Holy Catholic Church has survived despite bad decisions by government officials, lack of support from supposedly Christian nations and persecution from Communists. You will see how Our Lord's promise that "the gates of hell shall not prevail" against His Church are being fulfilled.

I hope that my efforts to make Mrs. Carroll's text more useful to you will help you to truly be all that God wants you to be for the Church. May God make clear to you, through the gifts of the Holy Spirit (especially Knowledge, Wisdom and Understanding), the history of His world and Church that you are about to study. I will be praying for you and I ask your prayers for me. God bless you.

—Mrs. Belinda T. Mooney

## Contents

## Timeline of Major Events in the History of the Americas

| | |
|---|---|
| B.C. 1000 | **Olmecs begin human sacrifices** (approximate date). |
| A.D. 1200 | **The Inca Empire established** (approximate date). |
| 1450 | **The Aztec tribe becomes powerful.** Tlacaellel mandates human sacrifice on a large scale (approximate date). |
| 1492 | **Columbus discovers the New World.** |
| 1513 | **Balboa becomes the first European to see the Pacific Ocean.** |
| 1521 | **Cortés conquers the last Aztec emperor,** ending human sacrifice and devil worship. |
| 1521 | **Magellan accomplishes the first circumnavigation of the world.** |
| 1531 | **Our Lady of Guadalupe** appears to Juan Diego in what is now Mexico. |
| 1531-1548 | **9 million Indians in Mexico become Catholics.** During the same time period, approximately the same number of Catholics are lost to Protestantism in Europe. |
| 1553 | **Father** (now Blessed) **Anchieta begins work in Brazil.** |
| 1575 | **St. Turibius is appointed Archbishop of Lima in Peru.** His work of evangelizing Peru is spiritually assisted by four Saints (St. Martin de Porres, St. Rose of Lima, St. Francis Solano and St. John Massias). |
| 1598 | **Spanish missionary activity** pushes north to New Mexico. |
| 1646 | **St. Isaac Jogues is martyred: one of the 8 Jesuit Martyrs of North America.** |
| 1763 | **French and Indian War** ends. |
| 1768-1784 | **Fr. Junipero Serra** evangelizes California. |
| 1773 | **The Boston Tea Party** |
| 1774 | **The Intolerable Acts** and **First Continental Congress** |
| 1775-1782 | **U.S. War for Independence** |
| 1776 | **U.S. Declaration of Independence** |
| 1789 | **George Washington becomes President,** as the French Revolution rages in France. |
| 1789 | **Fr. John Carroll is appointed to become the first bishop in the U.S.** |
| 1791 | **Adoption of the Bill of Rights** |

**1793** **First ordination of a Catholic priest on U.S. soil** (by Bishop John Carroll).

**1803** **The Louisiana Purchase** doubles the size of the U.S.

**1809** **St. Elizabeth Ann Seton founds the Sisters of Charity,** the first American religious order.

**1812** **The War of 1812**

**1820** **John England becomes the first Bishop of Charleston;** later establishes the first Catholic newspaper.

**1846-1848** **The Mexican War**

**1836-1860** **St. John Neumann ministers in America,** especially in Philadelphia.

**1861-1865** **U.S. Civil War**

**1867** **Emperor Maximilian** is executed in Mexico, marking the real beginning of the Revolution in Mexico.

**1874** **Garcia Moreno** is assassinated by revolutionaries after working to restore Ecuador's Catholic heritage. Radical liberals come to power in Ecuador in 1895.

**1898** **Spanish-American War**

**1910** **The Revolution in Mexico**—its "formal" beginning

**1917** **Our Lady of Fatima appears;** the **Russian Revolution** takes place.

**1914-1918** **World War I,** which the U.S. enters in 1917. As a result of the War, and largely through President Woodrow Wilson, Communism under Stalin gains control over many Catholic nations in eastern Europe.

**1927** **Bl. Miguel Pro's** martyrdom in Mexico proclaiming *Viva Cristo Rey!*

**1929-1939** **The Great Depression** (approximate dates), with the Stock Market Crash taking place in 1929.

**1933-1945** **Franklin Roosevelt's terms** as President. **The New Deal** programs fight the Depression and give the federal government much control over American life.

**1939-1945** **World War II,** which the U.S. enters at the bombing of Pearl Harbor in 1941; ends with atom bombing of Hiroshima and Nagasaki by U.S.

**1945** **Founding of the United Nations**

**1949** **The People's Republic of China** (Red China) is set up, ruled by the Communist Mao Tse-tung.

**1950-1953** **Korean War**

*Continued . . .*

**1952-present** **Moral decline in America,** assisted by the Warren Court, liberals in universities, etc.

**1956** **Hungarian Freedom Fighters** die as U.S. denies them aid; Hungary falls to Communism.

**1959** **Fidel Castro takes control of Cuba** on January 1.

**1962-1965** **Vatican Council II;** Liberals seize the opportunity to spread Liberal ideas as "the spirit of Vatican II."

**1965-1973** **War in Vietnam;** Vietnam falls to Communism in 1975.

**1968** ***Humanae Vitae*** (papal encyclical) reaffirms the intrinsic immorality of contraception.

**1973** ***Roe v. Wade*** declares all laws prohibiting abortion to be unconstitutional; abortion takes the lives of 1½ million U.S. babies per year by the mid-1980s.

# CHRIST AND THE AMERICAS WORKBOOK

*and Study Guide*

—With Answer Key—

# 1 THE NEW WORLD MEETS THE OLD

Text Pages 1-18

**Perfect Score: 100** **Score:** ________________
(Each Question is worth 2 points.)

## Completion

**Directions:** Complete and make each statement true and accurate by writing one or more words on each blank line.

1. The change in human life by which men began to grow their own crops and raise animals rather than only hunting and gathering food occurred in the New World around 2500 B.C. and is called the ______________________ Revolution. This contrasts with the Old World's achievement of this change around 9000 B.C.
2. After the overthrow of Quetzalcoatl, human sacrifice returned and the society of the Toltec people became ______________________ , with the individual person being of little importance.
3. The Aztecs' chief gods were the Hummingbird Wizard and Tezcatlipoca, and their religious symbol was the ______________________ .
4. Tlacaellel was so immoral and bloodthirsty that at the mass murder dedicating a new temple to the Aztec ______________________ gods, he ordered and watched 80,000 men be killed in four days.
5. Inca rule under Pachacuti and his son Topa Inca extended over the immense area from northern Ecuador to central ______________________ , an area of over 350,000 square miles.
6. The island of Samana City in the Bahamas was probably the first island Christopher Columbus reached; after thanking God and claiming the land for Spain, he named the island ______________________ , which means Holy Saviour.
7. Columbus made a total of ______________________ voyages from Spain to the New World between the years of 1492 and 1504. He died two years later, not having reached the Indies, but having opened up the West to the Catholic culture of Europe.

8. At this time period, the strength of the Catholic Faith in Europe was most evident in Spain, which was ruled by ______________________ and ______________________, who were known as *los Reyes Católicos*—"the Catholic Kings."

9. The Spaniards who colonized the New World in South and Central America built a ______________________ society continuing to this day and influencing even the U.S.A. in the names of cities such as San Francisco, San Antonio and Santa Fe.

10. After Pedro Cabral's discovery of ______________________ in 1500, Portugal regularly sent ships to the New World to continue to explore.

11. The Treaty of Tordesillas (1494) gave Spain the right to explore west of the imaginary Line of ______________________, an area consisting of most of North and South America, while Portugal was allowed the eastern part of South America.

12. In his remarkable exploration of the continental United States, while searching for the alleged "Fountain of Youth," the Spaniard Juan Ponce de Leon discovered the Gulf Stream and land which is now the state of ______________________, becoming the first white man to explore what is now the continental U.S.A.

13. ______________________ was the Caribbean island which Diego Velazquez colonized in 1511. This was the base from which expeditions to Mexico were later sent.

14. ______________________ is the man whose name was given to the new continents, even though he lied about making a voyage there in 1497 and was not one of the first Europeans in the New World, as he claimed.

## Multiple Choice

**Directions:** After each statement below, there is a set of words or phrases. Circle the letter next to the one word or phrase that best completes the sentence.

1. The staple crop around which life revolved in the New World was not known in the Old World. It was:
    a) wheat
    b) corn
    c) potatoes
    d) sweet potatoes
    e) none of the above

2. All of the following were part of the Mayan civilization, except:
   a) abolition of human sacrifice
   b) advanced mathematics
   c) excellent astronomy
   d) development in irrigation

3. According to a prophecy, Quetzalcoatl would return in the year:
   a) 2-Reed
   b) 3-Reed
   c) 1496
   d) none of the above

4. The Inca culture of Peru included:
   a) written communication
   b) a highly developed governmental system
   c) beautiful architecture
   d) b and c only
   e) a, b and c

5. The highly organized society of the Incas, in which individuals existed to serve the government, was structured as a:
   a) circle
   b) pyramid
   c) hexagon
   d) triangle

6. The first known European colonies in the New World were those of:
   a) St. Brendan the Voyager
   b) Christopher Columbus
   c) the Vikings
   d) the Phoenicians

7. The ship of Columbus that ran aground on a coral reef was the:
   a) Niña
   b) Pinta
   c) Santa María
   d) none of the above

8. Portugal's Prince Henry, who wanted to find a new route to the Indies and further the Kingdom of God, financed many voyages down the African coast, giving his men his vision and courage, until finally in 1498 they were successful. He was known as:
   a) The Navigator
   b) The Voyager
   c) The Sailor
   d) The Zealous

9. To follow up on earlier discoveries, Portugal sent three ships to Brazil in 1501 under the command of:
    a) Amerigo Vespucci
    b) Gonáclo Coelho
    c) Pedro Cabral
    d) none of the above

10. The leader of the second Spanish expedition into Mexico, during which the Spaniards first realized that the Aztecs practiced human sacrifice, was:
    a) Hernan Cortés
    b) Diego Velazquez
    c) Vasco da Gama
    d) Juan Grijalba

## True/False

**Directions:** Circle the letter T if the statement is true or F if the statement is false.

| | | | |
|---|---|---|---|
| 1. | T | F | The New World was not far behind the Old World in beginning to grow crops and raise animals. |
| 2. | T | F | The Aztecs were the first civilization to offer human sacrifices. |
| 3. | T | F | The difference between a civilization and barbarism is the presence of cities and the ability to write; the Mayan civilization in Central America and southern Mexico was the first civilization. |
| 4. | T | F | The eighteen-month year that the Mayans developed is slightly more accurate than our present-day calendar. |
| 5. | T | F | Montezuma I was the most powerful man in the Aztec Empire during his reign, effectively ruling the Aztecs for 67 years. |
| 6. | T | F | The first white child to be born in the New World was born to Thorfinn and Gudrid Karlsefni, Vikings who attempted to form a colony on the northern tip of Newfoundland. |
| 7. | T | F | Christopher Columbus was born in Portugal in 1451. |
| 8. | T | F | Queen Isabel wrote a letter in Spanish to the King of China—to be delivered through Christopher Columbus, even though she was not sure the King would be able to read it. |
| 9. | T | F | The second voyage of Christopher Columbus, in 1493, resulted in the discovery of Venezuela. |
| 10. | T | F | Columbus was primarily motivated to bring Christ to people who did not know Him, for the glory of God. |

11. T F The third voyage of Columbus, in 1498, was to Cuba; this was his first continental landfall in the New World.

12. T F Columbus was as good an administrator as he was a navigator. Due to his good administration of the colonies, Isabel was very pleased with Columbus, especially with his treatment of the Indians.

13. T F Columbus' fourth voyage, from 1502 to 1504, was spent primarily in ensuring correct administration of the colonies.

## Matching

**Directions:** This list is made up of names of persons, groups, places and things. Each one corresponds to one of the lettered phrases below. In each blank, write the letter of the phrase that correctly identifies that person, group, place or thing.

1. ___ Central America
2. ___ Quetzalcoatl
3. ___ Tlacaellel
4. ___ Pachacuti
5. ___ St. Brendan (The Voyager)
6. ___ Tim Severin
7. ___ Eric The Red
8. ___ Bjarni Herolffson
9. ___ Palos
10. ___ Charles I
11. ___ Vasco da Gama
12. ___ Manuel
13. ___ Vasco Nuñez de Balboa

A) Spanish port near Seville from which Columbus sailed on his first voyage (September, 1492)
B) Irish Saint; reached Newfoundland in a leather boat in the 6th century
C) first European (a Spaniard) to see the Pacific Ocean
D) Toltec leader who abolished human sacrifice and reformed religion for a time
E) first man to reach India in 1498 by an all-water route around Africa
F) established colony in Greenland in 985
G) one of the greatest Inca emperors; ruled in 1438
H) oldest village sites in the New World (dating from around 2000 B.C.)
I) Isabel's grandson; defended the Church against Protestants and Moslems
J) warrior Aztec ruler for 67 years—oversaw the sacrifice of over 50,000 humans per year
K) King of Portugal; married to Maria (Isabel's daughter); authorized Cabral's journey
L) Irishman who duplicated St. Brendan's voyage in the 1970s
M) first Viking to reach a continental landfall (at Newfoundland)

**Mini-Essay Question:** (Extra credit—4 points.) Describe two key aspects of the inherently unjust Aztec society as described in the text.

**Personal Opinion:** Name an important or interesting fact that you learned in this chapter. How could this fact affect your life?

**Supplemental Reading**

William Thomas Walsh. *Isabella of Spain: The Last Crusader*. TAN.

Warren H. Carroll. *Isabel of Spain: The Catholic Queen*. Christendom Press, Front Royal, Virginia.

# 2 TWO HEROES: CORTÉS AND MAGELLAN

Text Pages 20-33

**Perfect Score: 100**
(Each Question is worth 2 points.)

**Score:** ________________

## Completion

**Directions:** Complete and make each statement true and accurate by writing one or more words on each blank line.

1. Although his 300 Spaniards faced an empire of ______________________ Aztecs, Cortés was determined to succeed, stating that the greater were the obstacles, the greater would be the glory.

2. Cortés' banners bore these words: "Brothers and companions, let us follow the sign of the Cross with true ______________________, and in it we shall conquer."

3. Cortés' first request for supplies was not for crossbows or muskets, but for ______________________ and altar wine.

4. The sacrifice of humans was so widespread that one of Montezuma's buildings near the temple at Tenochtitlán was constructed of mortar and ______________________.

5. Panfilo Narvaez's intention to march against Cortés in April of 1520 was motivated primarily by ______________________ for the gold of the Aztecs. His action had grave consequences: while Cortés was putting down Narvaez's revolt, the Aztecs besieged his men.

6. On the "Night of ______________________," along with most of their horses, half of the Spaniards were killed when the Aztec warriors attacked as the Spaniards tried to leave Tenochtitlán, and nearly every remaining Spaniard was wounded.

7. After three months of warfare, and reinforced by ______________________ allies, the Spanish army captured the temple pyramid of the devil gods and destroyed it, burning everything in it.

8. Born in Portugal in 1480, Ferdinand Magellan was a very devout Catholic; after his request for command of a ship was denied by King Manuel of Portugal, he took service with ______________________, the King of Spain at that time.

9. Magellan was commissioned by the King of Spain to be Captain General of an expedition to find a water route through ______________________, then to continue on to the East Indies from there.

10. Magellan dedicated his trip, which set sail with five ships from San Lucar, Spain in 1519, to Our Lady of ______________________; due to the opposition of the Spanish captains, the voyage was very difficult for Magellan.

11. The name that Magellan gave to Rio de Janeiro was Santa ______________________ Bay, in honor of the Saint whose feast day it was when he landed there on December 13, 1519. About this time, Magellan put down a third mutiny attempt.

12. The ______________________ of Magellan were so difficult to navigate, due to storms, that when Magellan reached the Southern Sea, he named it "Peaceful"—the Pacific Ocean.

13. When Magellan reached the country called the ______________________ in 1521, he accomplished the first circumnavigation of the world, since he had sailed past these same islands 9 years earlier. Due to Magellan's good influence, the King and other natives accepted Baptism.

14. The ______________________ Islands, the original destination of Magellan's expedition, were reached by his men in 1521, after Magellan's unfortunate death in April. Only 108 men survived and reached these islands, although five ships had begun the voyage.

## Multiple Choice

**Directions:** After each statement below, there is a set of words or phrases. Circle the letter next to the one word or phrase that best completes the sentence.

1. An Aztec legend set the Aztec year 1-Reed and the day 9-Wind for the return of their hero:
   a) Tenochtitlán
   b) Quetzalcoatl
   c) Zocotlan
   d) Montezuma

2. When Cortés christened the town Villa Rica de Vera Cruz (Rich Town of the True Cross), he claimed which country in the name of Charles I of Spain?
   a) Mexico
   b) Cuba
   c) San Salvador
   d) Ecuador

3. The tribe which planned to ambush Cortés and his Spaniards were the:
   a) Zocotlans
   b) Cholulans
   c) Tlaxcalans
   d) none of the above

4. Cortés did many daring things in his conquest of the Aztecs, including:
   a) taking Montezuma prisoner in his own palace
   b) marching into the temple, striking and removing the idols
   c) fighting Cuitlahuac when outnumbered twenty to one
   d) a and b only
   e) a, b and c

5. After praying for assistance from Our Lady, St. James and St. Peter, the Spanish killed the Aztec general and prevailed against the Aztecs in the critical Battle of:
   a) Otumba
   b) Tlaxcala
   c) Tenochtitlán
   d) Cholula
   e) none of the above

6. Tlaxcala was the location where Cortés planned the final battle and also:
   a) helped his men recover (most were wounded)
   b) secured surrounding territory
   c) ordered the building of ships
   d) a and b only
   e) a, b and c

7. In May of 1521, when Cortés began the final battle at Tenochtitlán, the Spaniards fought constantly for:
   a) 36 days
   b) 39 days
   c) 63 days
   d) 93 days
   e) none of the above

8. The name of Magellan's flagship was the:
   a) Santiago
   b) San Antonio
   c) Trinidad
   d) Victoria

9. Provisions from Spain for Magellan's voyage were inadequate, since the ships were supplied with enough for only:
   a) 6 months
   b) 1 year
   c) 2 years
   d) 3 years
   e) none of the above

10. After sailing through what seemed like endless seas, Magellan's starving crew finally reached this land of plentiful food in March of 1521:
   a) Guam
   b) St. Paul Island
   c) The Philippines
   d) The Spice Islands

## True/False

**Directions:** Circle the letter T if the statement is true or F if the statement is false.

1. T F Before the Spanish arrived, there were no horses in the New World.

2. T F Cortés massacred helpless, unarmed Indians in the battle with the Cholulans.

3. T F Montezuma listened attentively to, but did not understand, Cortés' explanation of God and his invitation for Montezuma to worship the One True God.

4. T F Cortés never fully realized the dangerous position he and his men were in at Montezuma's palace, since they were allowed to build a chapel and come and go as needed.

5. T F Montezuma removed the images of the devil gods in the temple after some hesitation, since he thought Cortés was Quetzalcoatl.

6. T F After Cortés slashed the curtain of the idols, Mass was said in the temple, which had before been dedicated to the Hummingbird Wizard and the Lord of Darkness.

7. T F Despite being outnumbered 50 to 500, Cortés' men managed to fight their way to the top of the 114-step temple in Tenochtitlán, destroy the idol there, set fire to everything that would burn, and fight their way back down again.

8. T F After the Night of Sorrow, Cortés was discouraged, thinking that perhaps his goal of winning Mexico for Christ could not be accomplished.

9. T F Cortés' men valued him so much that one of them gave up his own life to save Cortés from being caught and sacrificed during the assault at Tenochtitlán.

10. T F The capture of Cuauhtemoc on August 13, 1521, ended the reign of the devil gods and human sacrifice in Mexico. Spain had conquered by following the Sign of the Cross with true faith, as Cortés had said they would.

11. T F After the weather turned warm, Magellan and his men began the search for the waterway from the Atlantic to the Pacific which they called the *paso*.

12. T F After Magellan reached what he named Port St. Julian, the Spanish captains attempted mutiny again.

13. T F When the *Victoria* finally reached Spain on September 8, 1522, the spices it carried were sufficient to pay for Magellan's entire round-the-world voyage.

## Matching

**Directions:** This list is made up of names of persons, groups, places and things. Each one corresponds to one of the lettered phrases below. In each blank, write the letter of the phrase that correctly identifies that person, group, place or thing.

1. ___ Estremadura
2. ___ Bernal Diaz
3. ___ Marina
4. ___ Cactus Rock
5. ___ Witchywolves
6. ___ Panfilo Narvaez
7. ___ Good Friday
8. ___ Night of Sorrow/*Noche Triste*
9. ___ Cuitlahuac
10. ___ Juan de Salamanca
11. ___ Cuauhtemoc
12. ___ Juan de Cartagena
13. ___ Serrano

A) captain of the *Santiago* who helped find the *paso* (The Straits of Magellan)
B) Spaniard who fought Cortés in Mexico in 1520
C) time when Cortés and his men fled from Tenochtitlán under severe attack
D) Tenochtitlán—city of the devil gods; currently Mexico City
E) Hernan Cortés' birthplace in western Spain; very dry
F) killed Aztec general at Battle of Otumba

G) Spanish captain; arrested for mutiny against Magellan and marooned at Port St. Julian

H) Aztec emperor who lost Battle of Otumba to Cortés

I) when Cortés landed in Aztec territory

J) soldier in and chronicler for Cortés' expeditions

K) Aztec emperor who refused to surrender Tenochtitlán during a siege lasting 93 days; finally defeated by Cortés

L) Indian interpreter; warned Cortés about ambush planned by the Cholulans

M) the Spaniards' name for Huitzilopochtli

**Mini-Essay Question:** How were Cortés and Magellan alike as heroes?
(Extra credit—4 points.)

**Personal Opinion:** Name an important or interesting fact that you learned in this chapter. How could this fact affect your life?

**Supplemental Reading**

Warren H. Carroll. *Our Lady of Guadalupe and the Conquest of Darkness*. Christendom Press.

# 3 MISSIONARIES AND CONQUISTADORS

Text Pages 34-48

**Perfect Score: 100** **Score:** ________________
(Each Question is worth 2 points.)

## Completion

**Directions:** Complete and make each statement true and accurate by writing one or more words on each blank line.

1. After his conquest of the Aztecs, Cortés set up self-________________ towns in which Spanish and natives were integrated.
2. In 1524, the Mission of the ________________ put Franciscan priests in Veracruz for the first organized missionary activity in Mexico; over the next 250 years all Franciscan missionaries imitated their 200-mile barefoot walk to Mexico City.
3. The success of the Franciscan missionaries in converting so many Indians resulted largely from the doctrinal verses they taught the Indians, who loved ________________ and pageantry.
4. From the beginning of 1524 to the end of 1525, Mexico was without Cortés, who had gone to ________________ to personally stop a rebellion by another Spaniard.
5. Queen ________________, Charles I's wife and regent, appointed the second Audiencia in March of 1530, but it did not officially take over the government in New Spain until January 1531.
6. Since the devil can also cause apparitions, Bishop Zumárraga cautiously asked that the Lady from Heaven give a sign, so she caused Castillian ________________ to grow on the hillside in winter.
7. The lifelike image of Our Lady of Guadalupe has remained on Juan Diego's cactus fiber tilma since 1531, despite the fact that the cloth should have disintegrated in ________________ years.
8. The Indian ________________ that were developed by the early Spanish viceroys allowed the Indians to be protected, formally educated, taught the Catholic Faith, and to work. They formed the basis of Mexican society and have endured to this day.

9. When Francisco Vasquez de Coronado and his 36 men crossed into New Mexico on false advice from the Turk, they learned much about the inland territory, helping those who came after them to form colonies in New Mexico and ______________________ .

10. Hernán De Soto and his men explored Alabama, Mississippi and Tennessee before finally discovering the ______________________ River in 1541 and moving on through Oklahoma and Kansas.

11. Pizarro defeated the Incas at Cuzco, then founded ______________________, the capital city of Peru, in January of 1535.

12. Charles V sent Cabeza de Vaca to replace Pedro Mendoza in governing the ______________________ colonies in 1541. The settlers resented his policy against enslavement of the Indians, and after his return from establishing the colony of Los Reyes, they overthrew him.

13. In acknowledgment of the fact that ______________________ had prepared the way for Our Lady of Guadalupe to come to Mexico by first ridding the land of the worship of devil gods, Bishop Zumárraga extended him an invitation to the dedication of the first church on Tepeyac Hill on December 26, 1531.

14. At 62 years old, after endowing a convent, hospital and university, and imploring his heirs to return any land unfairly gained from the Indians, Hernán Cortés died in 1547. He was later buried in ______________________, as he had requested.

## Multiple Choice

**Directions:** After each statement below, there is a set of words or phrases. Circle the letter next to the one word or phrase that best completes the sentence.

1. Cortés' management of New Spain included the development of all of the following except:
   a) land
   b) slave trade of Indians
   c) agriculture
   d) self-governing towns

2. The hill on which Our Lady appeared to Juan Diego five miles north of Mexico City, which was once the site of an Aztec temple, was:
   a) Huejotzingo
   b) Veracruz
   c) Tepeyac
   d) none of the above

3. The first miracle of Our Lady of Guadalupe was the healing of:
   a) Juan Diego
   b) Juan Bernardino
   c) Bishop Zumárraga
   d) none of the above

4. The kind Viceroy of New Spain who would disguise himself and wander the city at night to discover abuses against the Indians was:
   a) Juan Vicente de Guemes
   b) Don Antonio de Mendoza
   c) Don Luis Velasco
   d) Bucarelil

5. In May of 1517, Panfilo Narvaez led an ill-fated expedition which resulted in several deaths and four men lost in the interior of North America. He began the expedition in:
   a) Veracruz, Mexico
   b) Athens, Georgia
   c) Cajamarca, Peru
   d) St. Petersburg, Florida
   e) none of the above

6. The city of gold in New Mexico which was promised to Coronado by the Turk, but which did not actually exist, was named:
   a) Cajamarca
   b) Asunción
   c) Quito
   d) none of the above

7. The Spanish leader who took 223 mounted men and 400 foot-soldiers through Georgia and the Carolinas, discovered the *Santo Espiritu* and then moved on through Oklahoma and Kansas was:
   a) Francisco de Coronado
   b) Hernán De Soto
   c) Francisco Pizarro
   d) Pedro Mendoza

8. The Spanish leader who collected a ransom of Inca gold and silver, and whose family unjustly ruled Peru through favoritism, oppression of Indians and other abuses was:
   a) Francisco de Coronado
   b) Hernán De Soto
   c) Francisco Pizarro
   d) Pedro Mendoza

9. Part of the time that Cabeza de Vaca governed Argentina was spent in an expedition from 1541-42 through a land with vampire bats and enormous ants, during which he and his men established the colony of:
   a) Los Reyes
   b) Quito
   c) Lima
   d) Buenos Aires

10. Orellana's men traveled down the Amazon in ships named the *Victoria* and the:
   a) San Francisco
   b) San Antonio
   c) San Salvador
   d) San Pedro
   e) none of the above

## True/False

**Directions:** Circle the letter T if the statement is true or F if the statement is false.

1. T F Cortés' decision to personally put down the rebellion in Honduras was beneficial, since no one else could have done the job.

2. T F Under Guzman, the first Audiencia of New Spain denounced slavery of Indians and high taxes.

3. T F The Mother of God told Juan Diego to tell the Bishop of her desire that a church be built where she could show how much she loved the Indians.

4. T F The name of Our Lady of Guadalupe is the name Our Lady gave herself when appearing to Juan Bernardino. Guadalupe was already a famous shrine in Spain.

5. T F Upon their return to Mexico City after a seven-year journey in North America, Cabeza de Vaca and his three companions looked the same as when they had left.

6. T F Andres da Campo and the two oblates survived, although Fr. Padilla was killed, and they finally returned to Mexico City five years after Coronado and the rest of his expedition had returned.

7. T F Francisco Pizarro executed the Inca Emperor, Atahualpa, in August of 1533, because Atahualpa did not fulfill his part of the bargain made.

8. T F God brought good out of the evil the Pizarros did in Peru; the Incas were no longer slaves and could now come to worship Christ.

9. T F *Santa Maria del Buen Aire*, which means St. Mary of the Good Air, was the colony which was founded in 1534 by Pedro Mendoza and is now Buenos Aires.

10. T F Cabeza de Vaca was rewarded for his just treatment of the Indians and good administration of the Argentine colonies.

11. T F Orellana fulfilled the request of his brother Gonzalo Pizarro to find food and return in 12 days, then undertook the trip with 60 men to explore the territory.

12. T F Orellana befriended the Indians throughout his journey through South America, always treating them as brothers.

13. T F Pizarro's expedition down the Amazon covered 6,000 miles of the most memorable sights.

## Matching

**Directions:** This list is made up of names of persons, groups, places and things. Each one corresponds to one of the lettered phrases below. In each blank, write the letter of the phrase that correctly identifies that person, group, place or thing.

1. ___ Francisco Vasquez de Coronado
2. ___ Don Antonio de Mendoza
3. ___ Marañon
4. ___ Pedro Mendoza
5. ___ Fray Martín de Valencia
6. ___ Baja
7. ___ Nuño de Guzman
8. ___ Alvar Nuñez Cabeza de Vaca
9. ___ Juan de Zumárraga
10. ___ Bucarelil
11. ___ Francisco de Orellana
12. ___ Don Luis Velasco
13. ___ Cristobal de Olid

A) Captain of the 1540 expedition through New Mexico and Texas for infamous city of gold, Quivira
B) second viceroy in Mexico; revered as a father
C) sailed down the Amazon across South America for 8 1/2 months
D) unjust chairman of the first Audiencia of New Spain
E) Franciscan missionary; leader of the first expedition for missionary purposes to New Spain
F) established first Argentine colony at what is now Buenos Aires; died at sea
G) name that Orellana's men called the Amazon River; they discovered it had tides and was so wide it looked like the sea
H) conquered Honduras; rebelled against Cortés
I) led 3 other Spaniards through Texas back to Mexico City after an absence of seven years
J) viceroy of Mexico who spent 10 hours a day at his desk to ensure work was done
K) Lower California; site of one of Cortés' exploratory expeditions
L) first viceroy in Mexico; heard Indian grievances one day each week
M) first Bishop of Mexico City; protector of the Indians of Mexico

**Mini-Essay Question:** (Extra credit—4 points.) Dispute the charges leveled against Cortés (greed, aggression, destruction of native culture) by examining his achievements as noted in the text.

**Personal Opinion:** Name an important or interesting fact that you learned in this chapter. How could this fact affect your life?

**Supplemental Reading**

Warren H. Carroll. *Our Lady of Guadalupe and the Conquest of Darkness*. Christendom Press, Front Royal, Virginia.

Francis Johnston. *The Wonder of Guadalupe*. TAN.

Fr. Robert J. Fox. *Saints and Heroes Speak*, Vol. 4, pp. 75-93 (St. Juan Diego). Fatima Family Apostolate.

# 4 BRINGING CHRIST TO THE NEW WORLD

Text Pages 50-64

**Perfect Score: 100** **Score:** ______________

(Each Question is worth 2 points.)

## Completion

**Directions:** Complete and make each statement true and accurate by writing one or more words on each blank line.

1. Along with Our Lady of Guadalupe, the Franciscans evangelized Mexico, while the ____________________ were missionaries to Brazil under the leadership of Father José de Anchieta.

2. Father Anchieta was called the ____________________ of Brazil because of his constant, tireless work to set up an Indian settlement, organize a college, bring about laws regulating slavery and even negotiate between warring tribes.

3. After 25 years of service (1553-1578), Father Anchieta was made the Jesuit ____________________ over all of Brazil. Additionally, his extensive writings led him to be called the Father of Brazilian literature.

4. St. Rose of Lima and St. Martin de Porres are good examples of how Catholics and other Christians can make reparation to God; they made reparation for sins committed against the Indians through prayer, doing acts of ____________________ almost unceasingly, and offering their sufferings to Christ.

5. Although St. Francis Solano was in Lima only eight years (1602-1610), he was known by all to be extremely holy and an excellent preacher. At his funeral, an extraordinary compliment to his holiness was paid by the Viceroy and the ____________________ of Lima, who both insisted on being pallbearers.

6. In 1610, nine years after the first colony had failed, the new governor of New Mexico moved it to a nearby mountain and named it ____________________ (Holy Faith), where it flourished.

7. Between the years 1600-1625, twenty-six Franciscans built ____________________ churches to help the Indians of New Mexico accept Christianity.

8. The Jumanos Indians, who were south of Albuquerque, and other Indian tribes related to Father Salas the appearance of a "lady in blue" who spoke to them of Christ and told them to beg for priests. Eventually Father Salas and Father ______________________ did go and baptize the Jumanos.

9. Following Father Anchieta's example in Brazil, the Jesuit ______________________ in Paraguay were isolated, self-supporting communities of Indians designed to protect and instruct them. From 1650 to 1720, they enjoyed a Golden Age, with abundant crops and Indians flocking to them.

10. The English and ______________________ were Spain's enemies and, unfortunately, their false and biased documents against Spain have been unquestionably accepted, leading many to believe that Spaniards are cruel, greedy and depraved, and almost always in the wrong.

11. The Spanish government did not allow Indians to be bought and sold as slaves (as were black people from Africa). While Spanish kings thought of the Indians as their subjects, who should be protected, the nation of ______________________ regarded them as enemies.

12. Although the Spanish colonies and Indian villages did not have free elections, they did have elected councils called ______________________; these worked to help keep the peace in the region ruled by Spain.

13. The ______________________ was propaganda that was spread with the specific purpose of ruining the reputation of Spaniards in the New World.*

14. The culture in the New World which Spain fostered was evidenced by the poets, painters, sculptors, musicians and forty colleges and universities that existed by 1800. Even eighty years before Harvard, the University of ______________________ was established in 1553.

* Note: This bias and deception is *very* common today in other texts on American and Latin American history. This is why it is so important to read history from reliable, Catholic sources and to share these sources with others.

# Multiple Choice

**Directions:** After each statement below, there is a set of words or phrases. Circle the letter next to the one word or phrase that best completes the sentence.

1. The settlement envisioned by Padre Nobrega to hold a Jesuit university and seminary later became:
   a) Rio de Janeiro
   b) Lima
   c) Santa Fe
   d) Sao Paolo

2. The priest who was present at the establishment of both Sao Paolo and Rio de Janeiro and who organized the Jesuit college at Rio was:
   a) Padre Nobrega
   b) St. Turibius
   c) Father Antonio Ruiz Montoya
   d) Father Anchieta
   e) none of the above

3. The courageous head of the Paraguayan missions who led 250 Indian families down the Paraná River and through the forest (500 miles total) to protect them from enemies was:
   a) Father Antonio Ruiz Montoya
   b) Father Juan de Salas
   c) Father Font
   d) Fray Junípero Serra
   e) none of the above

4. The Franciscan priest who was left lame from a poisonous bite on the foot assumed responsibility as president of the missions in Lower California in 1768. Through the nine missions he founded, 6,000 Indians were baptized and 4,500 Indians lived in the mission communities. He was:
   a) Father Antonio Ruiz Montoya
   b) Father Juan de Salas
   c) Father Font
   d) Fray Junípero Serra
   e) none of the above

5. The Spanish commander of the expedition to Lower California, whose mission was to settle the areas as far up the coast as possible before the Russians could expand, was the pious:
   a) Juan Bautista de Anza
   b) José de Galvez
   c) Diego Vargas
   d) none of the above

6. The Spanish leader of the 240 colonists who settled near Monterey, California, establishing the farming community of San José in 1776 was:
   a) Juan Bautista de Anza
   b) José de Galvez
   c) Diego Vargas
   d) none of the above

7. The Spanish leader who took 200 Spaniards back to New Mexico in 1692, resettled the area and reconverted the Indians was:
   a) Father Antonio Ruiz Montoya
   b) Diego Vargas
   c) Father Lopez
   d) José de Galvez
   e) none of the above

8. The Black Legend has as its theme(s):
   a) the Spanish killed millions of Indians
   b) the Spanish oppressed and enslaved the Indians
   c) the Spanish government in the New World was oppressive and unjust
   d) a and c only
   e) a, b and c

9. The Spanish are also blamed, though unjustly, for the spread of diseases which were fatal to Indians because of their lack of immunity, particularly:
   a) chicken pox
   b) scarlet fever
   c) smallpox
   d) measles

10. If the Spanish were as cruel as the negative propaganda made them out to be, there would have been terrible revolts against them. Instead, without professional soldiers or standing military forces, except on the frontier for protection, the Spanish peacefully governed the New World for:
   a) 50 years
   b) 100 years
   c) 200 years
   d) 300 years

# True/False

**Directions:** Circle the letter T if the statement is true or F if the statement is false.

1. T F Father José de Anchieta was the victim of an accident which dislocated his spine. Although he made great efforts and accomplished a great deal, the pain often prevented him from fulfilling his mission.

2. T F The path Father Anchieta called "the worst trail in the world" is now a highway which bears his name.

3. T F Both St. Martin de Porres and St. Rose of Lima had gifts for healing which led them to care for the sick. They made no distinction between races or illnesses.

4. T F The pirate Spillbergen was hired by Dutch Calvinists to terrify the people of Lima into surrendering their valuables without a fight.

5. T F St. Francis Solano befriended the Tucumán Indians, his first assignment; later, he was sent to Lima where he was known for his severe penances, powerful preaching and joyfulness.

6. T F St. Peter Claver (1581-1654) was a Spanish Jesuit who gave gifts of biscuits, brandy, tobacco and lemons to the Indian tribes he served.

7. T F After the Indians revolted in 1680 because the governors would not allow Indians the same rights as white men, as the Spanish government in Madrid had dictated, the Indians at Sante Fe knew a much better life under Chief Popé.

8. T F Charles III was a deeply religious man, like all of the Hapsburgs before him; he reorganized the government in the New World and helped society to become more compassionate and humanitarian.

9. T F The Bourbons believed in checks and balances on the king's power and local rights, as opposed to absolutism. They believed that the Church should prevail over the king and have the authority to judge his actions.

10. T F The catastrophic effect of the actions of the Marquis de Pombal and the King of Spain in expelling the Jesuits was the enslavement of the Indians or their return to the jungle, undoing the Jesuits' work.

11. T F *A Brief Relation of the Destruction of the Indies*, the book used by the enemies of Spain to spread the Black Legend, was written by Bartolomeo de las Casas, who overstated the plight of the Indians, citing the impossible figure of 20 million Indians killed by Spaniards.

12. T F Although the Spanish did import Negro slaves, their slave code was more humane than that of the English or French, and there were a large number of free black people in the Spanish colonies.

13. T F The Hapsburgs in Spain (rulers from 1515-1700) supported local rights.

## Matching

**Directions:** This list is made up of names of persons, groups, places and things. Each one corresponds to one of the lettered phrases below. In each blank, write the letter of the phrase that correctly identifies that person, group, place or thing.

1. ___ Padre Nobrega
2. ___ José de Anchieta
3. ___ Saint Turibius
4. ___ King Philip III
5. ___ St. Rose of Lima
6. ___ George Spillbergen
7. ___ St. Francis Solano
8. ___ St. Peter Claver
9. ___ Father Benevides
10. ___ Ven. Mary of Agreda
11. ___ Diego Vargas
12. ___ Marquis de Pombal
13. ___ Charles III

A) first white man to leave the Chaco alive; he became a hero in Indian folk songs
B) Spanish leader who went to Santa Fe in 1692 to resettle the area and reconvert the Indians
C) abolished Indian personal servitude; authorized Jesuits to convert Indians in Paraguay
D) Jesuit superior in Brazil; envisioned Jesuit university and seminary; arranged peace conference between warring Indian tribes
E) Spanish Jesuit missionary to black slaves in the Caribbean (Cartagena)
F) controlled government of Portugal during the reign of Joseph I; expelled Jesuits from Portugal and its colonies in 1759
G) led others in prayer and stood in front of Tabernacle to prevent pirates from committing sacrileges
H) missionary to Jumanos Indians; identified the "lady in blue" on a return visit to Spain
I) Bourbon King of Spain; expelled Jesuits from Spain and its possessions in 1767
J) appointed Archbishop of Lima in 1575; served people through poverty, prayer and penance; appealed to the King and the Pope for the Indians
K) pirate hired by Dutch Calvinists to attack churches in Lima; died of apoplexy
L) bilocated to the New World to teach Indians about Christ until priests could come; urged Indians to beg for priests
M) priest who was present at establishment of Sao Paolo and Rio de Janeiro; organized Jesuit college at Rio

**Mini-Essay Question:** (Extra credit—4 points.)

Identify:

1. The greatest benefit the Spanish brought with them to the New World, a benefit which it still enjoys today.
2. The greatest weakness of the Catholic missionary effort in the New World, as noted in the text.

**Personal Opinion:** Name an important or interesting fact that you learned in this chapter. How could this fact affect your life?

**Supplemental Reading**

Sr. M. Alphonsus. *St. Rose of Lima.* TAN.

Giuliana Cavallini. *St. Martin de Porres.* TAN.

Mary Fabyan Windeatt. *St. Francis Solano.* TAN.

Mary Fabyan Windeatt. *St. John Masias.* TAN.

Ven. Mary of Agreda. *The Divine Life of the Most Holy Virgin.* (From *The Mystical City of God.*) TAN.

Fr. Robert J. Fox. *Saints and Heroes Speak*, Vol. 2, pp. 27-33 (St. Martin de Porres). Fatima Family Apostolate.

Agnes Repplier. *Father Serra.*

# 5 FRANCE IN THE NEW WORLD

Text Pages 66-78

**Perfect Score: 100** **Score:** ____________

(Each Question is worth 2 points.)

## Completion

**Directions:** Complete and make each statement true and accurate by writing one or more words on each blank line.

1. Unfortunately, the French kings and prime ministers of the 16th and 17th centuries tried many times to undermine the power of Spain and the ____________ rulers of the Holy Roman Empire, despite the fact that all were Catholic.

2. Prince Edward Island was the French possession in New France that was founded by Champlain in 1603, which he originally named Isle St. ____________ .

3. The volumes of letters sent by the Jesuits to France beginning in 1625, which greatly publicized New France, were known as the ____________ .

4. To assist New France, Champlain gained the support of Prime Minister Richelieu, who organized the Company of 100 ____________ ; this financed the journeys of 300 colonists to New France each year and their support for three years.

5. Beginning in 1608, Champlain worked to build the colony of Quebec until the British conquered in 1629. Upon the colony's return to France in 1632, after France paid the dowry of Princess Henrietta Maria, who married King ____________ of England, Champlain devoted the last three years of his life to stabilize the colony.

6. When the Jesuits celebrated the farewell ____________ in anticipation of their martyrdom, the Indians were confused that instead of being afraid of demons, the Blackrobes were joyous about going to Heaven.

7. Fr. Jogues prayed to find out if it was God's will that he should escape from the Iroquois, since escaping meant he would no longer be able to offer up his ____________ for the Indians.

8. Upon his arrival in Rome, through a special ______________________ given by the Pope, Isaac Jogues was allowed to continue saying Mass, even though he had lost his thumbs during the terrible tortures of the Iroquois.

9. In 1646, Isaac Jogues and his companions were killed with tomahawks in what is now New York State by the ______________________, who were a branch of the vicious Iroquois.

10. With the eventual conversion of the Iroquois Indians came the Baptism of the brave who had killed St. Isaac Jogues and the holiness of Blessed Kateri Tekakwitha, who lived a life of chastity and ______________________ to God and who is the first Native American to be beatified.

11. The "______________________ Girls" were orphans or girls from large families brought to New France to marry French settlers. They were taught catechism and housekeeping by Marguerite Bourgeoys so that they would be prepared to raise children and help populate New France.

12. When the saintly Bishop Francis Xavier de Laval was dying of gangrene and was asked to say a few last words, his humble reply was, "They were Saints. I am a ______________________." He died in 1708, having served New France faithfully as Bishop for nearly 50 years.

13. During his journey with Louis Joliet down the Mississippi River, Father Jacques Marquette commented on the Mississippi River ______________________, which he thought were "monstrous fish." He later lived in the area now named Chicago, where he continued evangelizing the Indians.

14. When Robert de La Salle reached the Gulf of Mexico with 400 colonists, he unknowingly sailed past the mouth of the Mississippi River and settled them in Texas. It was not until 1699 that the first French colony in the Mississippi Valley was founded at ______________________, followed by Mobile in 1710 and New Orleans in 1718.

# Multiple Choice

**Directions:** After each statement below, there is a set of words or phrases. Circle the letter next to the one word or phrase that best completes the sentence.

1. In 1535, 11 years after Verrazzano's voyage to the New World, Jacques Cartier discovered a village known as Hochelaga, where the Indians thought he was a medicine man. This village eventually became the city of:
   a) Quebec
   b) Isle St. Jean
   c) Montreal
   d) Illinois

2. During his second expedition, Cartier and his men spent their first harsh Canadian winter in Quebec, where an Indian recommended eating the leaves of this type of tree to assist the men's recovery from scurvy:
   a) cypress
   b) sycamore
   c) oak
   d) birch
   e) evergreen

3. The first missionaries to New France, brought by Samuel Champlain in 1615, were:
   a) the Franciscans
   b) the Jesuits
   c) the Dominicans
   d) none of the above

4. Champlain's 32 years of dedicated work from 1603 to 1635 resulted in all of the following achievements except:
   a) establishment of fur trading
   b) establishment of a permanent colony
   c) the beginning of missionary work in New France
   d) maintenance of peace with all of the Indians

5. St. Isaac Jogues and his companions endured which of the following as part of their tortures from the Iroquois in 1642:
   a) fingers chewed
   b) the rack
   c) running the gauntlet
   d) a and c only
   e) all of the above

6. The Iroquois terrorized French settlers and other Indian tribes with weapons and ammunition supplied by France's enemies:
    a) the Spanish
    b) the Dutch
    c) the English
    d) the Portuguese

7. The hardships endured by the Ursuline nuns included:
    a) failure to build a school
    b) failure to raise money for a school
    c) constant coldness
    d) a and b only
    e) a, b and c

8. Bishop Francis Xavier de Laval helped Quebec to become a Catholic society by doing all of the following except:
    a) encouraging Godly laws
    b) setting up a seminary
    c) setting up schools
    d) saying the first Mass of the day at 4:30 a.m.
    e) administering Confirmation to the Iroquois chief

9. Count Louis de Frontenac, the governor general of New France from 1672-1682, appointed this man to explore the water routes beyond Lake Michigan in order to find a passage to the west:
    a) Giovanni Verrazzano
    b) Jacques Cartier
    c) Louis Joliet
    d) Robert de La Salle

10. The priest who accompanied La Salle and others aboard the *Griffin* through the Great Lakes and discovered St. Anthony's Falls (now Minneapolis), later taking all the credit for La Salle's explorations was:
    a) Father Louis Hennepin
    b) Father Anthony Daniel
    c) Father Charles Garnier
    d) Father Noel Chabanel
    e) none of the above

## True/False

**Directions:** Circle the letter T if the statement is true or F if the statement is false.

1. T F As a result of the French kings and prime ministers' negative influence in fighting other Catholic rulers, the majority of the French people had become disloyal to the Church.

2. T F Verrazzano's journey up the eastern coast of North America to Newfoundland was followed up before King Francis I was released from his capture by the army of Charles I.

3. T F Champlain's excellent relationship with the Huron and Montagnais resulted in fur trading that eventually led to business investments and the further development of the colony at Quebec.

4. T F Fr. Jean Brébeuf began his attempt to convert the Indians by living with them from 1625-1627 to fully comprehend their language, customs and beliefs.

5. T F The Indians of New France blamed the Jesuits for the smallpox epidemic which struck them.

6. T F After the tortures, St. Isaac Jogues was forced by the Iroquois to live through the winter with the Dutch, who hated him and mistreated him.

7. T F Although tortured through the gauntlet, burned and slashed on torture posts, and tortured in other ways, Fr. Brébeuf constantly encouraged the others to keep faith and look forward to the joy awaiting them in Heaven. He was eventually killed by scalping and had his heart torn out.

8. T F Altogether, six men were martyred in New France by the Indians.

9. T F Mother Marie of the Incarnation proved to be a great executive when the convent burned down, and she had to secure funds and oversee the building of a new one.

10. T F The government of France assisted the newly married couples in New France by giving them animals and giving bonuses to the families who raised certain crops necessary for survival.

11. T F Bishop Laval was the first bishop of New France; he arrived in Montreal on June 16, 1659.

12. T F Robert de La Salle persevered despite seemingly insurmountable obstacles, such as the betrayal of Fr. Hennepin and the sinking of the *Griffin*, which contained furs to pay his loan.

13. T F Because La Salle had never been to the mouth of the Mississippi and did not know what it looked like, upon his return to establish a colony, he continued on to the coast of Texas, establishing his colony there.

# Matching

**Directions:** This list is made up of names of persons, groups, places and things. Each one corresponds to one of the lettered phrases below. In each blank, write the letter of the phrase that correctly identifies that person, group, place or thing.

1. ___ King Francis I
2. ___ Giovanni Verrazzano
3. ___ Jacques Cartier
4. ___ Samuel Champlain
5. ___ Recollect Fathers
6. ___ Jean Brébeuf
7. ___ Isaac Jogues
8. ___ Mohawks
9. ___ Blackrobes
10. ___ Mother Marie of the Incarnation
11. ___ Marguerite Bourgeoys
12. ___ Blessed Francis Xavier de Laval
13. ___ Louis Joliet

A) founded the Ursuline school for French and Indian children in Quebec, which is the oldest convent school in North America

B) Father of New France; from 1603 until his death in 1635, he worked tirelessly to promote colonization in New France

C) travelled up the East coast of America (exploring Staten Island) looking for a shortcut to China

D) appointed by Count Louis de Frontenac to find a westward passage in the water routes beyond Lake Michigan

E) opened a boarding school and a vocational school for French and Indian children in Montreal; founded the Congregation de Notre Dame

F) leader of the first Jesuit missionaries to New France; nicknamed The Bear (Echon) because of his tall and powerful physique

G) name the Indians gave Jesuit missionaries to New France

H) commissioned voyages of Verrazzano and Cartier to the New World

I) his three voyages resulted in the discovery of Labrador, the Gulf of St. Lawrence, the St. Lawrence River and Quebec, and he attempted colonization in 1541

J) first Bishop of New France; served for nearly 50 years

K) nicknamed the Bird of Prey (Ondessonk) by the Huron Indians

L) branch of the Iroquois

M) branch of the Franciscans; first missionaries from France to the New World

**Mini-Essay Question:** List the names of the eight Jesuit martyrs of New France.
(Extra credit—4 points.)

**Personal Opinion:** Name an important or interesting fact that you learned in this chapter. How could this fact affect your life?

**Supplemental Reading**

Mary Fabyan Windeatt. *Blessed Marie of New France [Mother Marie of the Incarnation].* TAN.

Anne W. Carroll. *Christ the King—Lord of History*. (Material on Francis I, Charles I, Richelieu.) TAN.

Milton Lomask. *St. Isaac and the Indians*. Vision Books/Ignatius Press.

August Derleth. *Father Marquette and the Great Rivers*. Vision Books/Ignatius Press.

Evelyn M. Brown. *Kateri Tekakwitha: Mohawk Maiden*. Vision Books/Ignatius Press.

Martin J. Scott. *Isaac Jogues: Missioner and Martyr*.

Fr. Robert J. Fox. *Saints and Heroes Speak*, Vol. 1, pp. 148-159 (Bl. Kateri Tekakwitha). Fatima Family Apostolate.

# 6 FROM ENGLAND TO AMERICA

Text Pages 79-94

**Perfect Score: 100** **Score:** ________________

(Each Question is worth 2 points.)

## Completion

**Directions:** Complete and make each statement true and accurate by writing one or more words on each blank line.

1. Queen Elizabeth's hatred of ______________________ and the Catholic Church resulted in her challenging its power in the New World. She financed voyages of Sir Francis Drake who did great damage to the painstaking work this country had begun in the name of Christ.

2. The Lost Colony of ______________________ was never found. From 1587 to 1590, the colonists did not hear from England, and when a supply ship finally arrived in 1590, there was no one left.

3. The founding of Jamestown, Virginia with 105 people was accomplished in May of 1607 by the ______________________ Company.

4. John Rolfe assured the success of the colony at Jamestown by growing ______________________ as its main crop, which sold quickly in England. This made the colony self-supporting and thus assured the colony's success.

5. The General Assembly of 1619 was the first colonial ______________________ in the New World. This self-government through elected representatives would continue to the present day.

6. The written agreement titled the Mayflower ______________________ between the Saints and Strangers spoke of self-governance in the absence of the King and showed a reliance on the written word as law.

7. The rejection of tradition, monarchy and Church authority by the Saints resulted in the beginning of the basis for law in the New World, which relied on a ______________________ document or agreement as the ultimate authority.

8. The Puritans, who believed that they were the Elect and rejected all authority of the Church, were strongly anti- ______________________ .

9. Winthrop's vision of the Puritan community as a "city on a hill" (an example to other countries) began American ______________________, which is not true patriotism but a form of exaggerated nationalism, seeing America as better than other nations.

10. The colony of New Sweden established by the Swedish and Dutch in 1638 later became the state of ______________________.

11. Under the ______________________ of 1632, Charles I allowed Catholics to settle in Maryland under Cecil Calvert, second Lord Baltimore, and Leonard Calvert, the governor of the colony.

12. Wishing to prevent religious bigotry in the Maryland colony, Lord Baltimore introduced into the Maryland assembly The ______________________ Act in 1649, which granted freedom of worship to all Christians.

13. The outcome of the North American Wars between England and ______________________ was important because the victorious nation would determine the way North America would be developed. England had parliament, commerce, trading and Protestantism, while the other country had an absolute monarch, agriculture and Catholicism.

14. During the North American wars, England grew stronger materially and economically, while France and Spain weakened under the ______________________ kings.

## Multiple Choice

**Directions:** After each statement below, there is a set of words or phrases. Circle the letter next to the one word or phrase that best completes the sentence.

1. Though they did not like him, the colonists of Jamestown, Virginia mostly owed their survival to the determination of the President of the Council:
   a) John Smith
   b) John Rolfe
   c) William Brewster
   d) John Carver

2. The law passed by Parliament in 1593 requiring attendance at Anglican services, with the threat of imprisonment as its enforcement, was aimed at:
    a) Catholics
    b) Puritans
    c) Separatists
    d) a and c

3. The Saints, the congregation of Separatists from Scrooby, England, was under the leadership of:
    a) John Smith
    b) John Rolfe
    c) William Brewster
    d) John Carver

4. The Mayflower held 102 people including 38 colonists recruited by the merchant company, whom the Saints called:
    a) Calvinists
    b) Pilgrims
    c) indentured servants
    d) Strangers

5. The Puritan doctrine that man was corrupt and that government was the purifier of nations came from:
    a) John Calvin
    b) Martin Luther
    c) John Carver
    d) William Bradford

6. The written document used by the Puritans to set up and govern their "City on a Hill" was called:
    a) The Massachusetts Body of Liberties
    b) The Charter of 1632
    c) The Toleration Act
    d) none of the above

7. The Boston colony expelled many people who did not share their beliefs. This included a person who claimed that "saved" people could tell who the other saved people were and began declaring the state of salvation of everyone else. This person was:
    a) Roger Williams
    b) Anne Hutchinson
    c) Peter Minuit
    d) John Wheelwright

8. Chartered in 1732, the last of the original 13 colonies, which was founded by James Oglethorpe, was:
   a) Maryland
   b) Georgia
   c) South Carolina
   d) North Carolina

9. The British under General William Braddock were defeated at Fort Duquesne. After Braddock was killed, this man led the retreat back to Maryland:
   a) James Wolfe
   b) Marquis de Montcalm
   c) George Washington
   d) none of the above

10. The Treaty of Paris, signed in 1763, had this effect:
   a) Pontiac's Rebellion
   b) North America would be Protestant
   c) quarreling between colonies and England
   d) all of the above

# True/False

**Directions:** Circle the letter T if the statement is true or F if the statement is false.

1. T F Virginia was named in honor of Queen Elizabeth by Sir Walter Raleigh, whose ships landed there in 1584.

2. T F Sir Francis Drake attacked Spanish settlements along the west coast of South America, destroying their churches and other religious articles.

3. T F Sir Francis Drake became the third man to circumnavigate the globe when he sailed into Plymouth Harbor in 1580.

4. T F The primary reason for the failure of the London Company at Jamestown was because the colonists were lower class people who did not know how to farm.

5. T F Because he helped everyone work together to keep the Jamestown colony alive after its initial setbacks, Captain John Smith was well liked and admired, and he acquired much fame.

6. T F Separatists believed that church organization and central authority was good, but that each congregation should have its own doctrine.

7. T F The Puritans believed that government was the purifier of nations and that it represented a covenant with God; they also held a fundamental belief in man's corruption.

8. T F Under the Massachusetts Body of Liberties, Baptists, Quakers and Catholics were persecuted. Catholics were called children of the devil, and the Catholic Church was called "the Kingdom of Antichrist" by a leading Puritan preacher.

9. T F Maryland under Lord Baltimore was the first colony in which Catholics and Protestants lived peacefully, and St. Mary's church, founded by the Jesuits, was the oldest Catholic Church in the English colonies.

10. T F The primary reason for the founding of the colony of Georgia was to protect English land against the Spanish in New Orleans.

11. T F The Treaty of Utrecht (1713) resulted in Great Britain gaining the Spanish throne, Nova Scotia, Newfoundland and the Hudson Bay.

12. T F Pontiac's rebellion by the chief of the Ottawas was a valiant effort to oppose the English, who drove the Indians out of their lands.

13. T F The legacy left by England in the colonies included intolerance of Catholics, the belief that America was especially holy in God's eyes, trust in written documents and elected governments, and reverence for public education.

## Matching

**Directions:** This list is made up of names of persons, groups, places and things. Each one corresponds to one of the lettered phrases below. In each blank, write the letter of the phrase that correctly identifies that person, group, place or thing.

1. ___ John Cabot
2. ___ Sir Francis Drake
3. ___ Virginia Dare
4. ___ John Carver
5. ___ William Bradford
6. ___ John Winthrop
7. ___ Roger Williams
8. ___ Anne Hutchinson
9. ___ John Wheelwright
10. ___ Peter Minuit
11. ___ George Calvert
12. ___ William Penn
13. ___ Marquis de Montcalm

A) first English child born in New World; born at second colony of Roanoke
B) Quaker who founded Philadelphia with charter from Charles II
C) England's first explorer; landed in Newfoundland; lost without a trace
D) Second governor at Plymouth; celebrated October thanksgiving feast
E) governor of Puritans of Massachusetts Bay Company; wanted them to be "a city on a hill"
F) Separatist who founded colony at Providence, Rhode Island
G) English pirate sent by Elizabeth; attacked Spanish ships and towns
H) Lord Baltimore; established with his sons the colony of Maryland with Catholics and Protestants
I) founded New Hampshire colony
J) made governor of the Saints and Strangers through the Mayflower Compact
K) French commander in Canada who lost critical battle to England's James Wolfe
L) founded Newport, Rhode Island colony after banishment from Boston
M) purchased Manhattan Island from Indians; third governor of the Dutch colony there

**Mini-Essay Question:** (Extra credit—4 points.) Describe how Henry VIII's disobedience and defiance of Church authority led to English domination of North America and ultimately to the failure of the Maryland Experiment.

**Personal Opinion:** Name an important or interesting fact that you learned in this chapter. How could this fact affect your life?

# 7 EVE OF THE AMERICAN WAR FOR INDEPENDENCE

Text Pages 95-107

**Perfect Score: 100** **Score:** ________________

(Each Question is worth 2 points.)

## Completion

**Directions:** Complete and make each statement true and accurate by writing one or more words on each blank line.

1. The Stamp Act Congress convened delegates from nine of the 14 continental Colonies with ______________________ legislatures. Absent were Nova Scotia, North Carolina, New Hampshire, Virginia and Georgia.

2. Besides John Adams' nonviolent attitudes, he also advocated prudence and restraint. He believed in self-government in the Colonies and felt that this was already in place through the ______________________ granted by the King of England to each Colony.

3. The right to self-government was threatened by the Stamp Act and the ______________________ Acts, which levied taxes on goods, including tea, imported into the Colonies.

4. The colonists' name for the Boston Port Bill, the Massachusetts Government Act and the Quartering Act passed by the English Parliament in 1774 was the ______________________ Acts.

5. The delegates from Massachusetts at the First Continental Congress wrote the ______________________ Resolves, which stated that the Intolerable Acts and the Quebec Act were illegal and that people should take up arms against the British.

6. Deists such as Thomas Jefferson believed in God but not in the ______________________ of Christ, miracles, divine providence or personal relationships with God.

7. While John Adams believed in self-government for traditional and historical reasons, Jefferson advocated self-government on ______________________ grounds, which included the concept that each society must set up its own government, never bound by forms of government from the past.

8. The key figures at the Continental Congress included John Adams, Thomas Jefferson and Charles Carroll. Carroll was the only ______________________ to sign the Declaration of Independence.

9. Although Carroll's primary reason for supporting self-government was to preserve the rights of Catholics, he also opposed the Parliamentary acts because they usurped the rights which the original charter granted the citizens of the Colony of ______________________ .

10. Although the committee appointed to write the Declaration of Independence consisted of Adams, Jefferson and Franklin, ______________________ was actually the one who wrote the document from June 11 to June 28, 1776.

11. Changes to the final paragraph, deleting the part regarding the slave trade, and the addition of the phrase "with a firm reliance on the protection of divine ______________________ " to the last sentence were the only changes made by the Congress to the committee's draft of the Declaration of Independence.

12. Despite having enjoyed health, wealth, prosperity and public esteem, at the end of his life Charles Carroll said that what gave him the most satisfaction was the fact that he had practiced the duties of his ______________________ .

13. Liberalism was an outgrowth of the ______________________ Revolt, which rejected Church authority and made the individual conscience the sovereign judge of religious truth. Liberalism continued to develop in the 18th-century, when leading intellectuals of France, rejecting moral absolutes, authority and hereditary monarchy, sparked the French Revolution, with its overthrow of the French government, mob violence and dictatorship of terror.

14. Liberalism states that authority in government comes from the ______________________ , replacing the traditional understanding that authority comes from God.

# Multiple Choice

**Directions:** After each statement below, there is a set of words or phrases. Circle the letter next to the one word or phrase that best completes the sentence.

1. In 1767, Parliament taxed tea, paper, glass and painters' colors imported into the Colonies under the newly passed:
   a) Townshend Acts
   b) Boston Port Bill
   c) Massachusetts Government Act
   d) Quebec Act
   e) none of the above

2. The Parliament decision that followed the March 7, 1774 disposal of tea by the colonists and that resulted in the unemployment of many people, almost destroying their city, is known as the:
   a) Townshend Acts
   b) Boston Port Bill
   c) Massachusetts Government Act
   d) Quebec Act
   e) none of the above

3. The Parliament decision in 1774 which granted freedom of religion to Catholics, causing anti-Catholic fear and prejudice in the New England Protestants to resurface, was called the:
   a) Townshend Acts
   b) Boston Port Bill
   c) Massachusetts Government Act
   d) Quebec Act
   e) none of the above

4. Hoping to beat the British in reaching a certain strategic location on June 17, 1775, Americans mistakenly built fortifications at the wrong spot, where they could be easily surrounded. The erroneous location was:
   a) Bunker Hill
   b) Breed's Hill
   c) Dorchester Heights
   d) none of the above

5. The American Captain who issued the command, "Do not fire until you see the whites of their eyes!" due to the tremendously low supply of gunpowder was:
   a) John Pitcairn
   b) Henry Clinton
   c) John Burgoyne
   d) Israel Putnam
   e) none of the above

6. Although there were other losses, the first great military disaster to the Americans was under Benedict Arnold at:
   a) Lexington
   b) Bunker Hill
   c) Quebec
   d) Dorchester Heights

7. The person who defended the Declaration of Independence before the Congress as they debated it was:
   a) Richard Henry Lee
   b) John Adams
   c) Charles Carroll
   d) Patrick Henry
   e) Thomas Jefferson

8. The last surviving signer of the Declaration of Independence, who died at the age of 96 in the year 1832, was:
   a) Richard Henry Lee
   b) John Adams
   c) Charles Carroll
   d) Patrick Henry
   e) Thomas Jefferson

9. Liberalism, which is included in the Declaration of Independence, has to do with:
   a) rejection of moral absolutes
   b) a specific political philosophy
   c) rejection of authority and hereditary monarchy
   d) a and b only
   e) a, b and c

10. Liberal philosophy, as found in the writings of French intellectuals, was adapted to the circumstances in America by Americans, including:
    a) Thomas Jefferson
    b) Ben Franklin
    c) Patrick Henry
    d) a and b only
    e) a, b and c

## True/False

**Directions:** Circle the letter T if the statement is true or F if the statement is false.

1. T F When Parliament passed the Stamp Act to pay off debt accumulated during the long war with the French, the Colonies objected to this tax because it affected goods shipped out of the Colonies to England.

2. T F Many Bostonians were killed by the British soldiers when the Bostonians dumped tea into the harbor. This incident became known as the Boston Massacre.

3. T F The First Continental Congress resulted in a decision of the Colonies not to use or import any British goods until the Intolerable Acts were repealed.

4. T F The Minutemen were given their name because they were trained within a few minutes.

5. T F The taking of Quebec by colonial forces under the command of Israel Putnam failed due to harsh weather conditions, including heavy snow.

6. T F Massachusetts, which had been settled by Puritans, was democratic and made up mostly of fishermen, farmers and shopkeepers; whereas, Virginia was founded by Anglicans and was inhabited by aristocrats and plantation owners.

7. T F Thomas Jefferson believed in divine providence.

8. T F Jefferson's document entitled "Summary View of the Rights of British Americans," which denied Parliament any authority in colonial affairs, was written while he was a representative in Virginia.

9. T F Charles Carroll rejected the legitimacy of the English parliamentary government because King James II, although overthrown by William of Orange during the so-called Glorious Revolution in 1688, had still been the legitimate King of England.

10. T F The *ad hominem* arguments proposed by Dulaney in 1773 assisted Charles Carroll in repudiating the anti-Catholic laws of Maryland within three years.

11. T F The Carrolls, Benjamin Franklin and Samuel Chase successfully persuaded the Canadians to join with the Colonies against England.

12. T F The Declaration of Independence was offically adopted on July 1, 1775.

13. T F The French Revolution carried to the logical conclusion liberal philosophy's emphasis on freedom to overthrow government—by violence, when necessary.

# Matching

**Directions:** This list is made up of names of persons, groups, places and things. Each one corresponds to one of the lettered phrases below. In each blank, write the letter of the phrase that correctly identifies that person, group, place or thing.

1. ___ Hendrick Fisher
2. ___ Christopher Gadsden
3. ___ Samuel Adams
4. ___ Patriots
5. ___ Loyalists
6. ___ John Adams
7. ___ Paul Revere
8. ___ Henry Clinton
9. ___ Patrick Henry
10. ___ Daniel Dulaney
11. ___ Charles Carroll
12. ___ Richard Henry Lee
13. ___ Thomas Jefferson

A) wrote articles in *Maryland Gazette* as "first citizen" to refute new tax laws

B) radical Virginian; stated "give me liberty or give me death."

C) deist whose liberal philosophy made its way into the Declaration of Independence

D) delegate who first stated that all colonists should simply be thought of as Americans

E) wrote articles in *Maryland Gazette* as "second citizen" to defend new tax laws

F) leader of the Sons of Liberty in Boston

G) German immigrant farmer and delegate from New Jersey

H) colonists who rejected Parliament's authority and wanted colonial self-rule

I) Virginia delegate; introduced congressional resolution for free and independent states

J) colonists who believed in Parliament's authority and supported England

K) British general that stated "another such victory would have ruined us."

L) defended British soldiers' right to self-defense as inalienable

M) rode from Boston to warn Patriots that British troops were marching

**Mini-Essay Question:** (Extra credit—4 points.) State three tenets of the political philosophy of liberalism, and state the central fact regarding all authority which liberalism ignores.

**Personal Opinion:** Name an important or interesting fact that you learned in this chapter. How could this fact affect your life?

**Supplemental Reading**

Fr. Felix Sarda y Salvany. *Liberalism Is a Sin*. TAN.

# 8 THE UNITED STATES' WAR FOR INDEPENDENCE

Text Pages 109-120

**Perfect Score: 100** **Score:** ________________

(Each Question is worth 2 points.)

## Completion

**Directions:** Complete and make each statement true and accurate by writing one or more words on each blank line.

1. The two kinds of troops under Washington's command were the ______________________ Army, who were paid by Congress, and a group of militiamen who came directly from the individual colonies.
2. Although Washington wanted to evacuate and burn the city of Manhattan Island, ______________________ would not permit him to do so. The British inevitably attacked again and the Americans retreated a second time.
3. George Washington divided his army into ______________________ sections in his anticipation of the approach of the British.
4. The evacuation of Fort ______________________ on November 20, 1776 was so quick that there was not time to disassemble tents or put out fires under cooking food.
5. On December 13, 1776, General ______________________ was captured by the British while eating breakfast after failing to return to Washington with his troops. General Sullivan returned his troops to Washington to reunite the army.
6. Despite a number of military mistakes, Washington's courage and perseverance turned the war around on ______________________ night of 1776 with a surprise attack on the British.
7. Conditions at Valley Forge in the winter of 1777 got so bad that Washington wrote to Congress of the army's three choices if Congress did not provide provisions for the army: starve, dissolve, or ______________________ .
8. The victory at Saratoga, New York was critical in France's recognition of the United States as an independent nation; a treaty of alliance was signed on December 17, 1777, making France under King ______________________ the first government to assist the Americans.

9. Although General Lafayette's surprise attack in October of 1781 against the British failed, he did manage to capture two British ______________________ (small fortifications).

10. The message received by General Washington from Lord ______________________ on October 17, 1781 involved the surrender of York and Gloucester.

11. In August of 1782, British General Sir Guy ______________________ asked Washington to negotiate surrender terms with him; the British evacuated New York the following December.

12. The American War for Independence was won because of the steadfastness of ______________________, the British failure to press their advantages, and the assistance of the French.

13. A revolution is a total upheaval in government, ______________________, and way of life (order). Since this did not take place, the term American War for Independence is a more accurate description for the war than The American Revolution.

14. After the war, Washington rode back to his home in Mount ______________________, hoping to retire.

## Multiple Choice

**Directions:** After each statement below, there is a set of words or phrases. Circle the letter next to the one word or phrase that best completes the sentence.

1. Among Washington's problems with troops was/were:
   a) smallpox
   b) desertions
   c) shortage of arms
   d) b and c only
   e) a, b and c

2. The location where the British troops first landed to begin the war with the United States was:
   a) Long Island
   b) Brooklyn
   c) Manhattan Island
   d) Staten Island
   e) none of the above

3. Before Washington was able to turn the war around, he had been defeated in all major battles since leaving:
   a) Boston
   b) Manhattan Island
   c) Brooklyn
   d) New Jersey
   e) none of the above

4. Washington's surprise attack on the British at Christmas of 1776 resulted in surrender by the Hessians, mercenary troops from:
   a) France
   b) Germany
   c) England
   d) Scotland
   e) a European coalition

5. Washington's second victory, in January of 1777, was gained after marching through muddy roads and outflanking Cornwallis' troops in the Battle of:
   a) Brandywine
   b) Germantown
   c) Saratoga
   d) Princeton
   e) none of the above

6. The largest city in America at the time of September 1777, a city which the British entered without opposition, was:
   a) Saratoga
   b) Philadelphia
   c) Princeton
   d) Brooklyn
   e) none of the above

7. In the summer of 1780, because of its strategic position, Washington wanted to strengthen the Fort at West Point, which was located in:
   a) Pennsylvania
   b) Massachusetts
   c) Georgia
   d) Connecticut
   e) none of the above

8. Benedict Arnold's revenge against the American government for lack of recognition involved allowing a fort to deteriorate and corresponding with British General Clinton regarding the military situation at:
   a) Saratoga
   b) Philadelphia
   c) West Point
   d) Germantown
   e) none of the above

9. The French fleet came to Washington's rescue in August of 1781 with 28 ships and 3000 troops, which allowed Washington to corner Lord Cornwallis and secure the victory at:
    a) Boston
    b) Yorktown
    c) West Point
    d) Saratoga
    e) none of the above

10. The Americans' victory in their war for independence was due to:
    a) the British failure to press their advantages
    b) the assistance of the French fleet
    c) Washington's perseverance
    d) b and c only
    e) a, b and c

## True/False

**Directions:** Circle the letter T if the statement is true or F if the statement is false.

1. T F As the colonial leaders were signing the Declaration of Independence in Philadelphia, George Washington was in North Carolina overseeing problems associated with his troops.

2. T F George Washington once made the statement during the war, "such is my situation that if I were to wish the bitterest curse to an enemy on this side of the grave, I should put him in my place."

3. T F When Washington divided his army into sections, General Lee was his most trusted officer.

4. T F After the victory against the British at Christmas of 1776, a turning point in the war, many American troops stayed to serve past the expiration date of their enlistment.

5. T F The Battle of Brandywine at Chad's Ford on September 11, 1777, was one of the few successes for the Americans, as they outflanked the British.

6. T F General Benedict Arnold was given credit for the victory at Saratoga, New York against General Burgoyne on October 14, 1777.

7. T F The strategic location of the French fleet off Chesapeake Bay was important to Washington because it meant that he would have time to let his troops rest and regroup.

8. T F After the Battle at Yorktown, there were only a few minor battles at Charleston and Wilmington before the end of the war.

9. T F Washington fully realized that he could not have won the victory at Yorktown without the help of the French fleet.

10. T F Washington tried to persuade Congress to keep up the struggle and warned them not to become overconfident after the victory at Yorktown.

11. T F The Americans and British signed a treaty of peace, with Great Britain recognizing the Colonies' independence, on November 30, 1782.

12. T F The War for Independence is an example of great American military strategy and tactics.

13. T F The term American Revolution is an accurate description of the war because moral standards and civil order were destroyed in it and the Americans' way of life changed.

## Matching

**Directions:** This list is made up of names of persons, groups, places and things. Each one corresponds to one of the lettered phrases below. In each blank, write the letter of the phrase that correctly identifies that person, group, place or thing.

1. ___ Sir William Howe
2. ___ General Charles Lee
3. ___ General Burgoyne
4. ___ Horatio Gates
5. ___ Baron von Steuben
6. ___ Marquis de Lafayette
7. ___ General Henry Clinton
8. ___ Admiral D'Estaing
9. ___ Count Rochambeau
10. ___ Major General John Andre
11. ___ Admiral De Grasse
12. ___ Admiral Graves
13. ___ Lord Cornwallis

A) American commander; given credit for victory at Saratoga; deserted at Camden

B) Frenchman who commanded American troops; attempted surprise attack at Yorktown

C) surrendered positions of York and Gloucester after defeat at Yorktown

D) French commander who took French fleet to West Indies after losing the battle at Savannah

E) carried messages from Benedict Arnold to British General Clinton

F) British General who marched down from Canada and attacked at Saratoga

G) French commander who landed in July 1780 with 6,000 troops

H) British commander defeated by French fleet at Chesapeake Bay

I) Washington's subordinate officer; arrested for disobedience and misbehavior

J) replaced British General Howe

K) Prussian; trained and disciplined troops at Valley Forge

L) British General who did not press his advantage after the battle at Brooklyn

M) French commander who assisted Washington at Chesapeake Bay with 28 ships and 3,000 troops

**Mini-Essay Question**: (Extra credit—4 points.) Explain why the phrase "American War for Independence" describes America's war against England in the late 1700s more accurately than the terms "American Revolution" or "Revolutionary War."

**Personal Opinion:** Name an important or interesting fact that you learned in this chapter. How could this fact affect your life?

# 9 THE BIRTH OF THE AMERICAN GOVERNMENT

Text Pages 122-131

**Perfect Score: 100** **Score:** ______________

(Each Question is worth 2 points.)

## Completion

**Directions:** Complete and make each statement true and accurate by writing one or more words on each blank line.

1. In the original Articles of Confederation of 1777, the states had most of the power and the ______________________ was subservient to them.
2. In the beginning, since there were no ______________________ courts, there was no way to force the states to provide the money needed to carry on the national government.
3. In order to pay for the expenses of the war, Congress either ______________________ money or printed paper money. There was huge debt at both the national and state levels of government.
4. Because of the choice between two opposing and completely different forms of government—whether to have a form of the existing Confederation, or a national government whose power rested in the central government—the years from 1783 to 1787, during which this decision was made, is called the ______________________ Period in American History.
5. Shays' Rebellion was caused by farmers trying to force the Massachusetts Legislature to deal with economic problems. ______________________ used the rebellion to try to change the Confederation.
6. The ______________________ Convention was the Federalists' attempt to plan a totally new government with power and authority resting at the national level, even though many others who supported the Convention believed that all that was necessary was to amend the Articles of Confederation to meet the new needs of the country.
7. The ______________________ Compromise was adopted, against the wishes of James Madison, so that the smaller states would not be constantly outvoted by the larger states. It allowed one house of the legislature to have proportional representation, while the other had equal votes for each state.

8. In order to ratify the Constitution, each state had to hold a ______________________, which would vote upon it, and when seven states had voted in favor of it, the Constitution would be considered ratified.

9. The ______________________ *Papers* were written by Jay, Madison and Hamilton to encourage the states to ratify the Constitution.

10. In the beginning, the checks and balances system of the Constitution was similar to that of the ______________________ governments of the Middle Ages, such as Isabel's Spanish government and that of the Holy Roman Empire.

11. The serious flaw of the Constitution was the fact that it placed ______________________ (the source of authority) in the people and not in God, an idea that came from 18th-century liberalism.

12. In Christian societies, as opposed to the United States, the ______________________ was the ultimate check on governmental power.

13. Although the U.S. Constitution sets forth a sound governmental system, it allows matters of truth and ______________________ to become open questions, based on majority opinion and not anchored to Divine law. The checks and balances of the Constitution can then be subverted or ignored.

14. The writers of the Constitution set up the system called the ______________________ College to elect the President and Vice President of the United States.

## Multiple Choice

**Directions:** After each statement below, there is a set of words or phrases. Circle the letter next to the one word or phrase that best completes the sentence.

1. The Articles of Confederation, approved by the Continental Congress in 1777, set up a Confederation of the different states that would be governed by:
   a) an Electoral College
   b) a Congress
   c) the President
   d) none of the above

2. The earliest problems faced by the new government in America were primarily:
   a) disputes over land boundaries
   b) problems in foreign affairs
   c) problems regarding slavery
   d) economic problems

3. Gold or silver used as a form of payment was also referred to as:
   a) hard money
   b) specie
   c) debtor funds
   d) a and b only
   e) a, b and c

4. The leader of the Confederation who said that talking to the States about money was like preaching to the dead was:
   a) Alexander Hamilton
   b) John Hancock
   c) Robert Morris
   d) Daniel Shays
   e) none of the above

5. The proposal of a three-part system of strong national government—a national executive, a legislature and a judiciary—with authority over the States, which was introduced at the Constitutional Convention in 1787, was called the:
   a) Virginia Plan
   b) Connecticut Compromise
   c) Federalist Papers
   d) New Jersey Plan

6. The counterproposal, which would have retained and modified the Confederacy—a union of independent states, with certain powers being delegated to Congress for business that transcended state boundaries—failed by a vote of 3 to 7. This counterproposal was called the:
   a) Virginia Plan
   b) Connecticut Compromise
   c) Federalist Papers
   d) New Jersey Plan

7. The Federalists at the Constitutional Convention wanted general wording in the Constitution regarding the grant of power to the federal government, so that the federal government's power would be less restricted. The anti-Federalists wanted the federal government's powers to be specifically enumerated. The compromise was that a specific list of the new government's powers was included in the Constitution, but in order to carry these powers out, the government was given the authority to make all laws that were:
   a) "fitting and proper"
   b) "necessary and proper"
   c) "appropriate"
   d) "within reason"

8. A fundamental flaw and contradiction in the Constitution, which was supposed to guarantee human rights, involved the denial of the humanity of:
    a) illegal aliens/immigrants
    b) slaves
    c) unborn children
    d) none of the above
    e) a, b and c

9. Those against the ratification of the Constitution when it came to a vote in the states included:
    a) those with commercial and manufacturing interests
    b) wealthy landowners
    c) some original Patriots such as Samuel Adams and Patrick Henry
    d) b and c only
    e) a, b and c

10. The Constitution divided power between/among:
    a) legislature, executive and judiciary
    b) the President and his cabinet
    c) state and national governments
    d) a and c only
    e) a, b and c

## True/False

**Directions:** Circle the letter T if the statement is true or F if the statement is false.

1. T F The Confederation originally consisted of 10 colonies.

2. T F Legislative power is law enforcement.

3. T F Originally, the Congress' purpose was to carry on the War, handle foreign affairs and domestic affairs such as the disposition of lands to the west of the states' boundaries.

4. T F One of the most difficult aspects about the repayment of debt after the War was the disagreement between debtors and creditors about how the debt would be paid. Debtors wanted to pay in gold or silver while creditors demanded paper currency.

5. T F Farmers had a hard time paying the debt levied by the state governments because they had only paper money.

6. T F Had a form of the Confederation been adopted, the national government would simply have been a representative of the states, with its authority delegated by the states.

7. T F When the Connecticut Compromise was adopted, the larger states were happy but the smaller states were dissatisfied.

8. T F In the Constitution, state laws were made supreme over federal laws.

9. T F The promise of a Bill of Rights assisted Madison and the Federalists in securing the final votes needed to ratify the Constitution in Virginia.

10. T F Madison and Jefferson believed that a government's authority comes from God.

11. T F If the majority consent to any law, it is a legitimate law.

12. T F Those in the United States today who believe that anything is justifiable if declared "constitutional" are neglecting to ask themselves whether a law is in harmony with natural law and the law of God, putting their faith in the Constitution instead.

13. T F The establishment of a national bank in 1791 helped to set the precedents of broad interpretation of the Constitution and of the national government's authority over the states.

## Matching

**Directions:** This list is made up of names of persons, groups, places and things. Each one corresponds to one of the lettered phrases below. In each blank, write the letter of the phrase that correctly identifies that person, group, place or thing.

1. ___ John Hancock
2. ___ Daniel Shays
3. ___ James Madison
4. ___ George Washington
5. ___ Delaware, Connecticut, Georgia
6. ___ New York, Massachusetts, Virginia
7. ___ Delaware
8. ___ John Jay
9. ___ Rhode Island
10. ___ Dr. Benjamin Rush
11. ___ John Adams
12. ___ Alexander Hamilton
13. ___ Thomas Jefferson

A) wrote the *Federalist Papers* with Madison and Hamilton; threatened that New York City might secede from the state
B) states that wanted each state to have same number of votes in the national legislature
C) Philadelphian who said that the Constitution, "has a thousand . . . things to recommend it"
D) Washington's Secretary of the Treasury; proposed national bank
E) led band of Massachusetts farmers to force state legislature to rescind tax-debt laws
F) first Vice President; Federalists' choice
G) became the leader of the faction known as Republicans
H) last state to ratify the Constitution
I) elected presiding officer of Congress in 1785; did not go to New York for sessions
J) states that wanted proportional representation in the national legislature
K) chairman of the Constitutional Convention; wanted a strong national government
L) the first state to ratify the Constitution
M) Federalist who dominated Constitutional Convention; Father of the Constitution

**Mini-Essay Question:** (Extra credit—4 points.) Did the Constitution's excellent system of checks and balances continue to work well in the 20th century
a) with regard to the states' power?
b) among the three branches of government?
Give an example to illustrate your answer to b).

**Personal Opinion:** Name an important or interesting fact that you learned in this chapter. How could this fact affect your life?

**Supplemental Reading**

Douglas Southall Freeman. *George Washington.*

# 10 CATHOLICS IN THE NEW NATION

Text Pages 132-143

**Perfect Score: 100** **Score:** ________________

(Each Question is worth 2 points.)

## Completion

**Directions:** Complete and make each statement true and accurate by writing one or more words on each blank line.

1. The one reference to religion in the Constitution has to do with not forbidding a person from holding ______________________ in the national government because of his religion.

2. The ______________________ Amendment of the Bill of Rights prohibits Congress from using tax money to support a particular religion; this referred to the national government; states could do whatever they liked.

3. ______________________'s Seminary opened in 1791 in Baltimore, assisting those who had been forced to leave France due to the French Revolution.

4. In 1791 John Carroll opened ______________________ University for the general education and preliminary training of future priests.

5. After Prince Demetrius Gallitzin became a priest, he introduced himself as Father ______________________, concealing the fact that he was a prince. Since the Prince had been taught by his father to scoff at religion, his conversion at age 17 shows the power of a mother's prayers and example.

6. With the ______________________ Purchase in 1803, the size of the diocese in America under Bishop John Carroll doubled.

7. Fr. Charles Nerinckx was appointed by Pope Pius VII to be the Apostolic ______________________ for Louisiana. He also founded, with the assistance of Mary Rhodes, the Sisters of Loretto at the Foot of the Cross in 1812.

8. Bishop Carroll strongly opposed ______________________, in which parish trustees thought they could hire and fire priests, because he knew that it undermined the authority of the Church hierarchy. Parish trustees attempted to take over in Philadelphia, Baltimore and other places, even delaying the reappointment of a Bishop for Philadelphia for six years.

9. Bishop Carroll may not have seen the danger that the policy of separation of Church and state had of leading to religious ______________________, the belief that one religion is as good as another, as well as to the belief that the Church should not interfere in politics.

10. Born in 1774 and married in 1794, Elizabeth Ann Seton had a special concern for the poor and needy and practiced a daily examination of conscience in her striving for perfection; she and her sister-in-law Rebecca were called the "______________________ Sisters of Charity" because of their works of charity, especially toward poor widows.

11. Despite constant pressure and opposition from family and friends, and her Episcopalian Minister Rev. Henry Hobart's attempts to get her to return to the Episcopalian faith, Elizabeth took the counsel of Fr. John ______________________ and entered the Catholic Church in 1805, in St. Peter's Catholic Church in New York City.

12. Just four years after she entered the Catholic Church, Elizabeth Seton established the first native American religious order, the Sisters of Charity, under the authority of Archbishop John Carroll; within the next year she contracted ______________________, from which she died 11 years later.

13. When Our Lady appeared to ______________________ in 1830 regarding the Miraculous Medal, she foretold the union of Elizabeth's American Sisters of Charity with the French Daughters of Charity, which came about in 1850.

14. The first great Irish Bishop in America, John England, began his work in 1820 as the first Bishop of Charleston. Among his many accomplishments was the publishing of ______________________, the first Catholic newspaper in the U.S.

## Multiple Choice

**Directions:** After each statement below, there is a set of words or phrases. Circle the letter next to the one word or phrase that best completes the sentence.

1. Among the things that John Carroll did as Vicar Apostolic of the United States was/were:

    a) undertake a report on the Church's condition in America
    b) request that Catholics be allowed to marry first cousins
    c) request permission to celebrate Sunday Mass in the afternoon
    d) b and c only
    e) a, b and c

2. The foundations established in the mission territory of Kentucky around 1812 included:
   a) the Dominicans
   b) the Jesuits
   c) the Visitation Order
   d) the Sisters of Loretto at the Foot of the Cross
   e) a and d only

3. Although it is controversial whether John Carroll's ideas on separation of Church and State were liberal, he was not liberal in his ideas on the following:
   a) mixed marriages
   b) loyalty to the Holy Father (papal supremacy and authority)
   c) opposition to Napoleon and Freemasonry
   d) a and b only
   e) a, b and c

4. Elizabeth Ann Seton established all of the following except:
   a) boarding school for girls
   b) free school for neighborhood children
   c) organization for poor widows
   d) home for those dying of tuberculosis

5. The president of St. Mary's College in Baltimore who encouraged Elizabeth Seton to found a society of women who would set up a school for girls in the Baltimore-Washington area was:
   a) Father DuBourg
   b) Father J. B. David
   c) Father John Dubois
   d) Father John England
   e) none of the above

6. Elizabeth Seton's order, the Sisters of Charity, was founded March 25, 1809, under the authority of Archbishop John Carroll and the first superior:
   a) Father DuBourg
   b) Father J. B. David
   c) Father John Dubois
   d) Father John England
   e) none of the above

7. The Sisters of Charity spread out, taking over an orphanage in 1814 and then making a foundation in 1817 in:
   a) Baltimore
   b) Boston
   c) New York
   d) a and c only
   e) none of the above

8. America's first native-born Saint, who was canonized in 1975, was:
   a) Archbishop John Carroll
   b) Mother Rose Duchesne
   c) Bishop John Neumann
   d) Bishop John England
   e) none of the above

9. The total number of hours that Mother Rose Duchesne spent praying daily for the success of her missionary work with the Indians was:
   a) 2
   b) 4
   c) 8
   d) 10
   e) none of the above

10. Bishop John England did all of the following except:
   a) set up the first seminary in the diocese of Charleston
   b) established the Sisters of Our Lady of Good Remedy
   c) said Mass and set up a school especially for blacks
   d) set up a book society and library
   e) traveled and preached a great deal

# True/False

**Directions:** Circle the letter T if the statement is true or F if the statement is false.

1. T F Because of the protection granted in the Bill of Rights' First Amendment, Catholics were guaranteed equal rights in the states.

2. T F John Carroll was a priest in the Franciscan order who organized an ecclesiastical structure for the Church in the United States.

3. T F Ben Franklin objected to the appointment of John Carroll as Vicar Apostolic of the United States because he feared that Carroll's authority would be temporal instead of spiritual.

4. T F George Washington was elected the first President of the United States just before John Carroll was appointed the first Bishop of the United States.

5. T F At the first national synod, called by Bishop Carroll in 1791, rules for mixed marriages were set because these had become a major problem due to the small number of Catholics in the United States.

6. T F The need to divide the original diocese of America became apparent to John Carroll as the population grew; Rome created new dioceses, with Bishop Carroll recommending the new see cities and prospective bishops.

7. T F Between 1794 and 1803, Elizabeth Ann Seton had five children, lost her father and father-in-law in death, suffered financial hardships in the family's business and became a widow while in Italy.

8. T F Elizabeth Ann Seton's conversion to Catholicism was due in a very large part to the example of her friends, the Filiccis, whose belief in the Real Presence of Christ in the Blessed Sacrament became her own.

9. T F Though Elizabeth Seton lived, "in the secret of the tabernacle," she did not neglect her duties.

10. T F The free school opened in February 1810 by Elizabeth Seton for neighborhood children, including blacks, was the first parochial school in the United States.

11. T F The deaths of Elizabeth Seton's sons in 1812 and 1816 were her greatest trials.

12. T F Mother Rose Duchesne possessed the virtue of obedience. Although she wanted to work among the Indians from the beginning, the Bishop did not allow it, so instead she concentrated on education through a boarding school, novitiate and orphanage until 1841 when she was finally allowed missions work.

13. T F The Indians named Mother Rose Duchesne the "woman who always works" because of the wonderful work she did among them in the missions.

# Matching

**Directions:** This list is made up of names of persons, groups, places and things. Each one corresponds to one of the lettered phrases below. In each blank, write the letter of the phrase that correctly identifies that person, group, place or thing.

1. ___ Bishop Briand
2. ___ John Carroll
3. ___ Pacificus
4. ___ Daniel Carroll
5. ___ Antonio Filicci
6. ___ William Seton
7. ___ Fr. Stephen Badin
8. ___ Leonard Neale
9. ___ Prince Demetrius Gallitzin
10. ___ Bishop John Cheverus
11. ___ Bishop Egan
12. ___ Bishop Flaget
13. ___ Bishop John Connelly

A) Italian Catholic who assisted John Carroll in requesting a bishopric from Rome
B) first Bishop of the new diocese of Boston; assisted Elizabeth Seton
C) Coadjutor Bishop appointed to run Georgetown University
D) was appointed Bishop of the U.S. by Pope Pius VI in 1789
E) first priest ordained in the United States; refugee from French Revolution
F) first Bishop of the new diocese of Philadelphia
G) Bishop of the new diocese of New York
H) pen name used by John Carroll to refute newspaper attacks on Catholics
I) first Bishop of the new diocese of Bardstown, Kentucky
J) helped shape the First Amendment to the Constitution
K) first priest trained in America; 2nd priest ordained in America
L) Quebec Bishop whom Catholics in Maryland and Pennsylvania asked not to come to administer Confirmation
M) assisted Carroll in corresponding with Rome through his commercial firm

**Mini-Essay Question:** (Extra credit—4 points.) State two evils that can result from the policy of "separation of Church and State."

**Personal Opinion:** Name an important or interesting fact that you learned in this chapter. How could this fact affect your life?

**Supplemental Reading**

Rev. Joseph Dirvin. *Mrs. Seton*. National Shrine of St. Elizabeth Seton, Emmitsburg, Maryland.

Annabelle M. Melville. *John Carroll of Baltimore: Founder of the American Catholic Hierarchy*.

Fr. Robert J. Fox. *Saints and Heroes Speak*, Vol. 2, pp. 140-146 (St. Elizabeth Seton). Fatima Family Apostolate.

# 11 THE FRENCH REVOLUTION AND THE NEW WORLD

Text Pages 145-158

**Perfect Score: 100** **Score:** ______________

(Each Question is worth 2 points.)

## Completion

**Directions:** Complete and make each statement true and accurate by writing one or more words on each blank line.

1. Saint Domingue is an island between ____________________ and Puerto Rico. At the time of the French Revolution it was half French and half Spanish.

2. The two classes of blacks existing on the island were the free people of color and the 450,000 ____________________ who worked on the plantations.

3. Napoleon desired to make Saint Domingue a base to build an overseas ____________________. He seized control of it in 1799.

4. The Republic of ____________________ was established after Napoleon withdrew his Army from Saint Domingue; the islanders had rebelled again after Toussaint's arrest.

5. The misconception that the ____________________ was similar to the American War for Independence, and therefore was a justified rebellion against a tyrannical king, gained American sympathies that have lasted to this day.

6. Washington kept the U.S. out of war by issuing a Neutrality Proclamation on April 22, 1793; this resulted in ____________________ resigning as Secretary of State, while James Monroe, U.S. ambassador to France, was recalled from France.

7. When the ____________________ Affair became known in October of 1797, Americans rallied behind Adams against the French.

8. Fearing war with France, in 1798 Congress passed the Alien Act and Alien Enemies Act to address the French citizens in the U.S. who were agitating against the government and the ____________________ Act to deal with the Republican newspapers that were attacking the government in support of the French.

9. The 6-day tie between Thomas Jefferson and Aaron Burr in the presidential election of 1800 led to official recognition of the ______________________ system.

10. In 1800, Vermont and Maryland voted for ______________________, who became president as a result of an announcement that this candidate would not abolish the Navy or eliminate the public credit system, both of which he had earlier promised to do.

11. ______________________ appointed the Federalist John Marshall as Chief Justice, whose ruling in the case of Marbury v. Madison on February 24, 1803 has been used by the courts to establish judicial supremacy even though this was not the intent Marshall had when writing it.

12. The ______________________ Act of 1789 was the law Marshall said could not be used in this case because it authorized an action that the Constitution did not allow.

13. Without the ______________________, armed vessels of private citizens licensed to pirate enemy merchant ships, the War of 1812 with the British could not have been won; they sunk many British ships, causing millions of dollars in damage.

14. The peace treaty ratified by the Senate on February 15, 1815, as the War of 1812 came to a close, assuring many that America would never be reconquered by the British, is known as the Peace of ______________________.

## Multiple Choice

**Directions:** After each statement below, there is a set of words or phrases. Circle the letter next to the one word or phrase that best completes the sentence.

1. All of the following happened during or as a result of the revolution on Saint Domingue except:
   a) Napoleon became disgusted with the attempt to maintain an empire in the New World
   b) Toussaint proclaimed himself Governor General for life
   c) Napoleon appointed Charles Leclerc to take over the island
   d) Toussaint surrendered his army and retired peacefully at his estate

2. The candidate in the presidential election of 1796 who was called a monarchist for distrusting the French Revolution was:
   a) Jefferson
   b) Adams
   c) Madison
   d) Monroe

3. Congress passed the Constitution's twelfth amendment providing for separate balloting for President and Vice President after the strange election of:
   a) 1808
   b) 1800
   c) 1796
   d) 1804

4. The Barbary War began when Thomas Jefferson refused to negotiate with pirates from the Barbary states. Although inexperienced, the U.S. Navy won the war, with the most important result being:
   a) U.S. advancement in world status
   b) Jefferson's increasing popularity among the citizens
   c) U.S. Navy receiving valuable experience
   d) Lieut. Stephen Decatur becoming a war hero

5. With Napoleon's desire to vacate the Western Hemisphere, Talleyrand, Livingston and Monroe finally negotiated the purchase of the Louisiana Territory, after much haggling, for the price of:
   a) $2 million
   b) $4 million
   c) $15 million
   d) $20 million
   e) none of the above

6. In the presidential election of 1808, the winner was a handpicked successor who led America into war with the British in 1812. He was:
   a) Jefferson
   b) Adams
   c) Madison
   d) Monroe

7. In 1814 the British attempted to win the War of 1812 through a three-pronged coastal attack—on Lake Champlain, New Orleans and:
   a) the Chesapeake Bay
   b) Boston harbor
   c) Fort Niagara
   d) Detroit

8. Among the ships owned by U.S. privateers that did much damage to British shipping during the War of 1812 was/were the following:
   a) the Argus
   b) the Yankee
   c) the Constitution
   d) a and b only
   e) a, b and c

9. The effects of the War of 1812 included all the following except:
   a) Federalist Party was strengthened
   b) American optimism and nationalism increased
   c) Andrew Jackson was made a national war hero
   d) none of the above

10. The overwhelming victory in the 1816 presidential election went to the prior Secretary of State:
   a) Jefferson
   b) Adams
   c) Madison
   d) Monroe

## True/False

**Directions:** Circle the letter T if the statement is true or F if the statement is false.

1. T F The Western Hemisphere was not affected by the French Revolution.

2. T F Jefferson's Republican party tended to support the policy of neutrality or favoritism toward Britain during the French Revolution, while the Federalists supported France.

3. T F Already by the election of 1800, the Electoral College had figured out how to manipulate the system of electing a president and vice president; this resulted in the electors voting a tie between Jefferson and Burr, which had to be decided by the House of Representatives (controlled by the Federalists).

4. T F The Tenth Amendment to the Constitution was written as a result of the election of 1800 to provide separate balloting for the Presidential and Vice Presidential races.

5. T F The reason that Marbury v. Madison is used to justify judicial supremacy is because Chief Justice Marshall said the Court could determine which laws Congress may pass.

6. T F The Embargo Act passed by Congress just prior to the War of 1812 with Britain forbade U.S. trade with foreign nations. Because this hurt the U.S. more than it did the British, Jefferson was unpopular and Americans did whatever was necessary to get around the law.

7. T F The British plot to provoke a revolution in New England was the final push toward war, and after Congress met on June 18, 1812, the war began. This occurred during the presidency of Jefferson.

8. T F The U.S. won three consecutive victories over the British naval force, even though Britain had been virtually unstoppable in its naval capacity for nine years.

9. T F After Oliver Perry's victory forced the British to evacuate Detroit, it was only a few months until Fort Niagara was regained as well.

10. T F Because Washington was the port of the privateers, it was a very strategic position that the British fought hard to capture.

11. T F Francis Scott Key wrote the *Star-Spangled Banner* while aboard a British ship as a prisoner. When Fort McHenry would not surrender, the British left Key there.

12. T F The people of England pressured the English government to win the war and not give up, since they were angry at the privateers depriving them of the goods they were waiting for in England.

13. T F Andrew Jackson took 2,500 volunteers, fed them on roots, berries and bark, and led them to victory over the British in the Battle of Lundy's Lane.

# Matching

**Directions:** This list is made up of names of persons, groups, places and things. Each one corresponds to one of the lettered phrases below. In each blank, write the letter of the phrase that correctly identifies that person, group, place or thing.

1. ___ Creoles
2. ___ *Grand Blancs*
3. ___ *Petit Blancs*
4. ___ Toussaint
5. ___ Talleyrand
6. ___ William Marbury
7. ___ John Marshall
8. ___ Lewis and Clark
9. ___ William Hull
10. ___ Isaac Hull
11. ___ William Henry Harrison
12. ___ Oliver Perry
13. ___ Andrew Jackson

A) commissioned by Jefferson to find the western boundaries of the Louisiana Territory
B) called himself *L'Ouverture*—"the opening"
C) defeated the British with 2,500 volunteers at New Orleans
D) American-born Spaniards
E) U.S. General who surrendered Detroit to the British in 1812 without firing a shot
F) wealthiest, most powerful Creole families on Saint Domingue
G) Commodore ordered by Madison to fight the British at Lake Erie
H) Federalist Chief Justice of the Supreme Court
I) commander of the *Constitution*; sailed out of port to avoid Madison's orders
J) France's devious foreign minister; a "former" bishop
K) middle-class families on Saint Domingue; tended to be liberal and racist
L) Major General sent to revitalize the Army and retake Detroit
M) filed suit in Supreme Court for the delivery of a writ of mandamus to Madison

**Mini-Essay Question:** (Extra credit—4 points.) Explain the doctrine of "judicial supremacy" and show how it allows the Supreme Court to, in effect, make "laws."

**Personal Opinion:** Name an important or interesting fact that you learned in this chapter. How could this fact affect your life?

**Supplemental Reading**

Professor Robin Anderson. *Pope Pius VII: His Life, Times and Struggle with Napoleon in the Aftermath of the French Revolution*. TAN.

# 12 SPAIN IS DRIVEN FROM LATIN AMERICA

Text Pages 160-170

**Perfect Score: 100** **Score:** ________________
(Each Question is worth 2 points.)

## Completion

**Directions:** Complete and make each statement true and accurate by writing one or more words on each blank line.

1. Besides being incited by liberal writings, the Creoles rebelled in Latin America because Charles III, of the ruling family of the ______________________ in Spain, raised their taxes, controlled their trade and eliminated local self-government (which the Hapsburgs had worked so hard to put in place).

2. Although the initial revolutions of the Creoles were suppressed and royal authority was restored in every country except ______________________ by 1815, the Revolution would continue.

3. The two major enemies of Francia that he sought to eliminate were the Creole aristocracy and the ______________________, whose lands he confiscated, whose income he took away and whose schools he closed.

4. Simón Bolívar declared the necessity of a centralized government because he did not believe that Latin America was ready for ______________________, even though he wanted liberty and independence.

5. The Battle of ______________________ in 1814 saw the defeat of General Olañeta and his troops. He was one of the few people in the terrible tragedy of Latin American independence who fought for the good of the people and the maintenance of their moral values.

6. After the royalists' defeat of Fr. José Morelos in Mexico in 1815, they established a ______________________ government, suppressing monastic and other orders and taking the property of anti-liberals.

7. The taking back of Mexico City from Iturbide, who called himself Emperor Agustín I, was accomplished in March of 1823 by Antonio Lopez de Santa Anna and General José Antonio ______________________, who replaced the dictatorship with a liberal republic.

8. Andrew Jackson accused the ________________________ Indians of making trouble, providing him with an excuse to invade Florida and take possession of the territory.

9. On February 22, 1819, the ________________________ Treaty was ratified as a result of Spain's concessions to the U.S., the end result being that the U.S. owned Florida and all disputed boundaries of the Louisiana territory. The only thing kept by the Spanish was Texas.

10. The ________________________ Doctrine delivered to Congress in December of 1823 was Adams and Monroe's attempt to stop European powers from intervening on behalf of Spain in Latin America. Unfortunately, this encouraged the leaders of the revolutions in Latin America.

11. The ________________________ Policy aligned the U.S. with Latin America by stating that any attempt by a European power to re-establish Spain in control in Latin America would be regarded as the manifestation of an unfriendly disposition toward the U.S.

12. Dom Pedro's impassioned cry: "The hour has come! Independence or death! We have separated from Portugal!" on September 7, 1822, is known to Brazilians as the "Cry of ________________________."

13. Dom Pedro II, who ruled Brazil for 49 years, was highly intelligent. He shared power with the professional classes and established peace and progress because he restrained within himself the desire for ________________________.

14. Independence in Latin America resulted in liberal governments with Creole aristocracy in power, the rapid growth of governmental ________________________, and ultimately inflation and economic decline due to the costs of these governments.

## Multiple Choice

**Directions:** After each statement below, there is a set of words or phrases. Circle the letter next to the one word or phrase that best completes the sentence.

1. The Creoles considered rebelling after Charles III began exercising tight control, and they were encouraged by the liberal writings of all of the following except:
   a) Voltaire
   b) Rousseau
   c) Jefferson
   d) Adams

2. In his effort to control the understanding Paraguayans had of the world, Francia did all of the following except:
   a) prohibit foreigners to enter the country without permission
   b) prohibit mail/trade
   c) outlaw newspapers and books
   d) outlaw slavery

3. Paraguay was a jail under Francia, as he refused to uphold traditional values and rightful authority for:
   a) ten years
   b) fifteen years
   c) twenty years
   d) twenty-five years
   e) thirty years

4. When Bolívar marched south from Bogotá in late 1821, he was trying to overtake the last province of New Granada:
   a) Ecuador
   b) Peru
   c) Venezuela
   d) Columbia
   e) none of the above

5. Though they were given land, without proper equipment, money and protection, this group of people in Peru fell into debt to local landowners and eventually became serfs:
   a) slaves
   b) Indians
   c) lower class Creoles
   d) none of the above

6. Agustín de Iturbide offered something for everyone in Mexico—including a constitutional monarchy, protection of the Church, and citizenship and equality for all citizens—in his plan known as the:
   a) *Plan de Comprehensia*
   b) *Plan de Iguala*
   c) *Plan de la Catolica*
   d) *Plan de Iturbide*

7. On September 27, 1821, Mexico City fell to the army of Iturbide, ending Spanish rule in Mexico, which had lasted for over:
   a) four centuries
   b) five centuries
   c) six centuries
   d) none of the above

8. After Dom Pedro I was forced to abdicate, a regent ruled Brazil for Dom Pedro II until he officially took control at the age of:
    a) 12
    b) 14
    c) 15
    d) 18
    e) 21

9. By the year 1830, all of Latin America was independent except for the islands of Puerto Rico and:
    a) Cuba
    b) Virgin Islands
    c) Grand Cayman
    d) none of the above

10. The governments set up by the Creole aristocracy were characterized in contrast to the Spanish by:
    a) power being exercised less wisely
    b) infighting among factions for power
    c) power being exercised with less restraint
    d) a and c only
    e) a, b and c

## True/False

**Directions:** Circle the letter T if the statement is true or F if the statement is false.

1. T F Uruguay did not break away from Buenos Aires and declare independence but Upper Peru did.

2. T F In 1823, Chile plunged into anarchy, but after seven years traditionalists took power and restored order and stability.

3. T F Once José de San Martín conquered Peru in 1821, it was not reconquered by the Spanish until 1830.

4. T F Though there was much bloodshed, the positive aspect of the wars of independence in the countries of Ecuador, Columbia and Venezuela was that the economies and crime rates improved.

5. T F Looking upon the Spanish King as their protector, the Indians in Columbia, Venezuela and Ecuador stayed out of the war.

6. T F The liberals helped the Indians by giving them the same rights as everyone else, and the Indians appreciated their own plots of land.

7. T F Initially, Bolívar could not see that he should cease the rebellion in Peru after it had become what he called a "chamber of horrors," but finally, at his death in 1830, he admitted that the revolts had been a failure.

8. T F Bolívar had a tricolor flag representing religion, independence and union.

9. T F Under Emperor Agustín I and the republic that followed his rule, the missions established in Mexico by Father Serra and the Franciscans flourished.

10. T F The Transcontinental Treaty between the U.S. and France resulted in the U.S. having more power over the North American continent.

11. T F The Monroe government gave diplomatic recognition to the new republics in Latin America, following the British and French's lead.

12. T F U.S. support for the revolutions in Latin America encouraged the rebels in their mistaken belief that a liberal republic was best, despite their experiences proving the contrary.

13. T F President Monroe, a protege of Jefferson, was pro-revolt and anti-Spain, but Secretary of State John Quincy Adams took after his father and opposed the revolutions in Latin America.

# Matching

**Directions:** This list is made up of names of persons, groups, places and things. Each one corresponds to one of the lettered phrases below. In each blank, write the letter of the phrase that correctly identifies that person, group, place or thing.

1. ___ Ferdinand VII
2. ___ José Gaspar Rodriguez de Francia
3. ___ José de San Martín
4. ___ Bernardo O'Higgins
5. ___ Simón Bolívar
6. ___ llaneros
7. ___ General Sucre
8. ___ Casimiro Olañeta
9. ___ Miguel Hidalgo
10. ___ José Morelos
11. ___ Dom Joao
12. ___ Dom Pedro I
13. ___ Dom Pedro II

A) atheist Creole aristocrat; led revolutions in New Granada, then Peru
B) traditionalist general; defeated in Upper Peru
C) Creole lawyer who won election of 1814 in Paraguay; Perpetual Dictator
D) became Emperor of Brazil after declaring Brazil's independence from Portugal
E) worked with Bolívar; president of Ecuador and Bolivia
F) supreme dictator of Chile; forced to abdicate in 1823
G) cowboys of Venezuela; assisted Bolívar in overtaking New Granada
H) Prince Regent of Portugal; proclaimed United Kingdom of Portugal and Brazil
I) mestizo priest who trained a small army in Mexico; defeated by royalists in 1815
J) led Army of the Andes with O'Higgins, then captured Peru
K) ruled Brazil 49 years in peace and progress following its independence
L) rightful King of Spain; deposed by Napoleon in 1808
M) liberal Creole priest who led peasant army of 60,000 in Mexico in 1810

**Mini-Essay Question:** (Extra credit—4 points.) After finally realizing that independence had not helped Latin America, Bolívar stated, "Independence is the only benefit we have gained, at the cost of everything else." Give three of the usual effects of the revolutions after the Spanish were overthrown and the new governments (liberal republics) were established.

**Personal Opinion:** Name an important or interesting fact that you learned in this chapter. How could this fact affect your life?

# 13 MANIFEST DESTINY

Text Pages 171-186

**Perfect Score: 100** **Score:** ________________
(Each Question is worth 2 points.)

## Completion

**Directions:** Complete and make each statement true and accurate by writing one or more words on each blank line.

1. When the Republican Party split into two groups, the Democrats were led by Jackson, while the ______________________ were led by Clay and Adams.

2. During the 1828 election campaign, supporters of Andrew Jackson screamed "corrupt ______________________ " at Adams, whose supporters in turn attacked the morality of Jackson and his wife, Rachel.

3. The Nullification Controversy during Jackson's administration was significant because South Carolina had threatened to ______________________ on account of its opposition to high tariffs.

4. Sam Houston received a secret commission from his friend President Jackson to determine whether or not ______________________ could be acquired by the United States, which was officially held by the country of Mexico. He crossed into this territory in December of 1832.

5. When the fortress known as the ______________________ was besieged by the Mexicans on March 6, 1836, all of the Texan soldiers inside it were killed.

6. Besides believing in manifest destiny, expansionists wanted to secure U.S. borders, allow legalized slavery in more states, assist land speculators and industrialists, and allow ordinary people to obtain ______________________ land to start a new life.

7. The idea that it was God's will that the U.S. expand to the Pacific Coast and control all of North America is known as ______________________, a term coined by *The United States Magazine and Democratic Review*.

8. Initially, President Polk did not listen to General Winfield Scott. However, Scott's plan for taking the port of ______________________, then moving on to Mexico City worked, and in September of 1847, the American flag was raised in Mexico City.

9. The first significant westward migration of settlers to ______________________ took place in 1843, and by 1846 the westward movement was very clear.

10. Joseph Smith claimed to have had a divine revelation ordering the practice of ______________________. This got him arrested and eventually killed while in jail.

11. The Mormons' two great assets were their sense of community and their leader, Brigham ______________________.

12. Franklin Pierce became President by gaining the sympathy of Americans for a wound received in the Battle of ______________________.

13. The Treaty of ______________________ ended the Mexican War in 1848 and gave the territories of New Mexico and California to the United States. This completed Manifest Destiny except for the small area of land in the Gadsden Purchase.

14. The year 1848 saw Americans debating the question of whether or not ______________________ would be allowed in the new territories acquired.

## Multiple Choice

**Directions:** After each statement below, there is a set of words or phrases. Circle the letter next to the one word or phrase that best completes the sentence.

1. The Spoils System, which is the replacement of government employees with one's own friends, was introduced on a large scale into the federal government by President:
   - a) Andrew Jackson
   - b) Martin Van Buren
   - c) John Tyler
   - d) James K. Polk
   - e) William Henry Harrison

2. After the military campaigns in 1813 and 1814, the Indians were pushed into the Southeastern states of Georgia, Mississippi and Alabama as the white settlers came to seize their lands. The primary tribes affected included all except:
   a) Cherokees
   b) Creeks
   c) Chickasaws
   d) Iroquois
   e) Choctaws

3. Giving generous loans to Congressmen, manipulating credit and calling in loans were all efforts to stall Congress in its vote not to recharter the U.S. bank, which happened in April 1833. The man responsible for this financial distress was:
   a) John Tyler
   b) Nicholas Biddle
   c) John Fremont
   d) Sam Houston
   e) none of the above

4. After the battle at San Jacinto—at which the victorious Houston had told his men: "Remember the Alamo!"—the losing General told Houston that he (Houston) had just defeated the "Napoleon of the West." The losing General who described himself thus was:
   a) General Winfield Scott
   b) Andrew Jackson
   c) Santa Anna
   d) Stephen Kearney
   e) Señor Castro

5. The president whose most significant act was signing the annexation bill which made Texas part of the United States was:
   a) Andrew Jackson
   b) Martin Van Buren
   c) John Tyler
   d) James K. Polk
   e) William Henry Harrison

6. The New Mexico territories that President Polk wanted to annex to the United States included the following states except:
   a) Nevada
   b) Utah
   c) Wyoming
   d) Colorado
   e) Idaho

7. The foreign capital conquered by U.S. troops under Stephen Kearney without a battle was:
   a) Santa Fe
   b) Houston
   c) San Antonio
   d) Brownsville
   e) San Angelo

8. America's talented general, Winfield Scott, was to have a career marked by the failure of a president and some subordinates to listen to him. When President Polk finally approved Scott's plans, Taylor deliberately disobeyed orders by trying to take his troops to this location:
   a) Veracruz
   b) California
   c) New Mexico
   d) Laredo
   e) none of the above

9. America's war with Mexico resulted in the following officer(s) receiving valuable training from General Scott:
   a) Zachary Taylor
   b) Robert E. Lee
   c) Ulysses Grant
   d) b and c only
   e) a, b and c

10. The Latter-Day Saints, also called Mormons, were founded by the writer of the *Book of Mormon*, which contains his supposed revelations. This person, who lived from 1805 to 1844, was:
    a) James Frazier Reed
    b) Brigham Young
    c) Joseph Smith
    d) Jacob Donner
    e) George Donner

## True/False

**Directions:** Circle the letter T if the statement is true or F if the statement is false.

| | | | |
|---|---|---|---|
| 1. | T | F | When John Quincy Adams became President, he was popular because of his honesty and his experience as Secretary of State. |
| 2. | T | F | The Cherokee Indians adapted to civilization and were peaceful. However, during Jackson's presidency, because they settled lands which white settlers wanted, state governments ordered them to surrender their lands and go to the Oklahoma territory, which they finally did in 1835. |

3. T F After Sam Houston resigned as Governor of Tennessee, he went to live with the Choctaw Indians in Alabama, having left his wife with her family due to disagreements.

4. T F Although he could have ordered Santa Anna's execution, Houston instead released him.

5. T F Presidential candidate Henry Clay ran on an expansionist platform in 1844, using the slogan "54-40 or Fight."

6. T F General Andrew Jackson earned the title "Old Rough and Ready" prior to his becoming President of the United States.

7. T F Although their territory had been civilized longer than that of the U.S., the Mexicans were portrayed as uncivilized and ignorant by the U.S. newspapers.

8. T F The volunteers who agreed to fight the Mexicans were subjected to lectures attacking the Mexicans' religion, Catholicism, and some French, Polish and Irish American Catholics called themselves the St. Patrick's Battalion and fought on the side of the Mexicans.

9. T F The Mexican men who fought the U.S., like their generals, were not very good fighters or very courageous.

10. T F After the Mormons settled the Great Salt Lake Valley, Utah was eventually admitted to the Union on the condition that polygamy be outlawed.

11. T F The Forlorn Hope referred to the men and women in the Mormon group who braved the journey to the Great Salt Lake Valley to help transform it.

12. T F Though James Reeds' family was finally reunited in California, all four of the Donner parents died.

13. T F When John Fremont was court-martialed for disobeying orders, he was severely criticized in the newspapers.

## Matching

**Directions:** This list is made up of names of persons, groups, places and things. Each one corresponds to one of the lettered phrases below. In each blank, write the letter of the phrase that correctly identifies that person, group, place or thing.

1. ___ Henry Clay
2. ___ John C. Calhoun
3. ___ Nicholas Biddle
4. ___ Sam Houston
5. ___ Martin Van Buren
6. ___ William Henry Harrison
7. ___ John Tyler

8. ___ James K. Polk

9. ___ John Fremont

10. ___ Robert Stockton

11. ___ Winfield Scott

12. ___ James Frazier Reed

13. ___ James Marshall

A) Commodore in command of the U.S. Fleet in California

B) first person to see a gold nugget in California; sighted gold at Sutter's Fort in 1848

C) Kentucky Senator who ran against Adams, Jackson and Crawford in the presidential election of 1824

D) Jackson's hand-picked successor from New York; President from 1837-1841

E) Vice President who became President from 1841-1845 upon the previous president's death

F) provoked Castro in California; assisted Stockton in occupying Los Angeles

G) leader of a group of pioneers migrating west; rode in the Prairie Palace Car

H) died after one month in office as President in 1841

I) Governor of Tennessee; commander-in-chief of the Armies of the Texas Republic

J) Vice President to Jackson; urged South Carolina to disobey protective tariff laws

K) most talented general in U.S. during Polk's presidency; victorious in Veracruz and Mexico City

L) Democratic nominee in 1844 whose slogan was "54-40 or Fight"

M) President of the U.S. Bank

**Mini-Essay Question:** List three of the reasons for "expansionist fever."
(Extra credit—4 points.)

**Personal Opinion:** Name an important or interesting fact that you learned in this chapter. How could this fact affect your life?

# 14 NO IRISH NEED APPLY

Text Pages 187-195

**Perfect Score: 100** **Score:** ________________
(Each Question is worth 2 points.)

## Completion

**Directions:** Complete and make each statement true and accurate by writing one or more words on each blank line.

1. ______________________ was an anti-Catholic movement in the 19th century; its participants attacked Irish Catholicism in the name of defending native American values.
2. The magazine, *The Protestant*, published in 1829, sought to "inculcate Gospel doctrines against Romish corruptions" and propagated the notion that Catholics could never be true Americans because of their allegiance to the ______________________.
3. Some of the earliest violence faced by Catholics at the hands of Nativists was in the city of Charlestown, Massachusetts with the burning of the ______________________ Convent, one of Boston's best schools.
4. In 1836, anti-Catholic books and publications distorted and blasphemed Catholic traditions by feeding upon the ______________________ of many Americans regarding Catholic customs, especially convent life.
5. In 1840, Bishop Hughes and others petitioned the Common School Society to allocate a share of ______________________ funds for Catholics; this was denied by the Society and again by the state legislature of New York.
6. Although the New York legislature abolished the Common School Society, they voted that public funds could not go to schools that taught any religious sectarian ______________________ or tenet.
7. Bishop John Hughes told his people that we Catholics "have for our mission to ______________________ the world—including the inhabitants of the U.S. . . ."

8. When the American Republican Party formed in June 1843, the platform was specifically ______________________, with one of its planks being a residency requirement of 21 years for immigrants to become citizens.

9. Native-born ______________________ not related to Catholics by blood or marriage were the only persons accepted into the Know-Nothings.

10. After his ordination, St. John Neumann first ministered in Buffalo, New York to about 400 ______________________ Catholic families who lived far apart.

11. Two times John Neumann blamed his spiritual inadequacy or lack of holiness for his problems. The first time resulted in him leaving New York to become a ______________________ novice in Pittsburgh; the second time he asked to be relieved as superior of the order.

12. John Neumann learned quickly that Protestantism and materialism dominated American culture; to protect his people, his top priority was Catholic ______________________.

13. John Neumann was made superior over the ten foundations of his order in America in 1847. Unfortunately, many priests were not responsive to his call to spiritual renewal and complained that he promoted ______________________.

14. The funeral procession for St. John Neumann, held in January of 1860, was the largest that the city of ______________________ had ever seen.

## Multiple Choice

**Directions:** After each statement below, there is a set of words or phrases. Circle the letter next to the one word or phrase that best completes the sentence.

1. Besides claiming that Catholics would never be true Americans, *The Protestant* also predicted which of the following:
   a) a new Vatican would be set up in New York
   b) Crusades throughout New England
   c) the Inquisition under Bishop John England
   d) none of the above

2. The anti-Catholic books published in 1836 included all of the following except:
   a) *Foreign Conspiracy against the Liberties of the United States*
   b) *Nun*
   c) *The Awful Disclosures of Maria Monk*
   d) *Six Months in a Convent*

3. *The Awful Disclosures of Maria Monk* was set in:
   a) a Visitation convent
   b) New York City
   c) Toronto, Canada
   d) Hotel Dungeon
   e) none of the above

4. Because of the prevailing anti-Catholic sentiment, the book by Maria Monk was a best seller. The number of copies sold prior to the beginning of the Civil War (in 1861) numbered:
   a) 50,000
   b) 100,000
   c) 200,000
   d) 300,000

5. The violence spurred on by Nativists resulted in all of the following happening in 1844 except:
   a) riots in Philadelphia
   b) blaming of Catholics and indictment of Irishmen who protected their homes
   c) riots in St. Louis
   d) burning of churches in New York

6. The anti-Catholic activities of the Know-Nothings in 1855 included:
   a) firing Catholic teachers in Philadelphia
   b) preventing Irish and German Catholics from voting in Louisville
   c) attempting to burn down a church in Brooklyn
   d) b and c only
   e) a, b and c

7. Irish Catholics responded to persecution with all the following except:
   a) humor
   b) expansion of parochial schools
   c) an exteme form of American nationalism
   d) bitter hatred for America

8. The happiest years of John Neumann's life were spent at St. James parish teaching catechism and instructing converts and working with immigrants in:
   a) Philadelphia
   b) Baltimore
   c) Pittsburgh
   d) Buffalo
   e) none of the above

9. In 1852, despite John Neumann's reluctance, he was appointed Bishop of:
   a) Philadelphia
   b) Baltimore
   c) Pittsburgh
   d) Buffalo

10. In addition to starting an order of nuns and founding a preparatory college for candidates to the priesthood, St. John Neumann began this devotion in his diocese:
   a) Sacred Heart
   b) Immaculate Heart
   c) Forty Hours
   d) Way of the Cross
   e) none of the above

## True/False

Directions: Circle the letter T if the statement is true or F if the statement is false.

1. T F While refused work (no Irish need apply), the Irish immigrants to the U.S. were blamed for being poor and were looked upon with hatred and prejudice.

2. T F The first phase of anti-Catholicism in the 19th century was an organized effort on the part of politicians to stir up hatred for Catholics mainly by word of mouth in Protestant churches.

3. T F The Nativism movement defended Native American Indian values against Irish Catholicism.

4. T F Maria Monk had been a resident in a small convent of nuns before meeting the local boy who became the father of her child.

5. T F The public schools in 1838 ridiculed Catholic children for their faith and contained passages in textbooks that were blatantly anti-Catholic.

6. T F When funds were not given to parochial schools, Bishop John Hughes went to his people asking for sacrifices to build their own schools. Even those who made six dollars a month contributed to build churches and the parochial school system in New York.

7. T F Daring John was Bishop Hughes' nickname because he dared to confront the violent forces and protect the churches in his diocese, even going so far as getting the mayor to cancel a mass meeting.

8. T F Whereas Nativism was initially unorganized, the second phase of anti-Catholicism moved to organized political activity in the 1840s.

9. T F When Irish people starved by the thousands in the potato famine of 1845, The U.S. responded with special collections and famine relief and welcomed the survivors who emigrated to the U.S.

10. T F The nickname "Know-Nothings" had to do with the pledge of the organization's members not to know any Catholics.

11. T F When the issue of slavery confronted the Know-Nothings, they were united against it.

12. T F The Americanist Heresy was condemned by Pope Leo XIII, and Catholic leaders in America affirmed their rejection of it at the time of the Pope's condemnation. However, the Americanist Heresy never fully died, and it reappeared after the Second Vatican Council.

13. T F Pittsburgh, like many other cities, felt the violent affect of Nativism when churches were burned, anti-Catholic publications were printed and priests were beaten when making sick calls.

# Matching

**Directions:** This list is made up of names of persons, groups, places and things. Each one corresponds to one of the lettered phrases below. In each blank, write the letter of the phrase that correctly identifies that person, group, place or thing.

1. ___ Samuel Morse
2. ___ Dr. William McCaffrey
3. ___ Maria Monk
4. ___ Father Phelan
5. ___ William K. Hoyt
6. ___ Hotel Dieu
7. ___ John Hughes
8. ___ Common School Society
9. ___ Order of United Americans
10. ___ Millard Fillmore
11. ___ Blood Tubs
12. ___ John Neumann
13. ___ Asa Symington

A) controlled funding for New York public schools; refused money to Catholic schools; was abolished in 1840s

B) 1856 presidential candidate nominated by the Know-Nothings

C) Canadian Protestant minister; tried to bribe Mrs. Monk to say her daughter had been a nun

D) Irish father trampled to death in anti-Catholic violence in New York City

E) gang who gruesomely tried to keep Catholics in Maryland from voting

F) one of the leaders of Know-Nothings; declared John Neumann an enemy of American institutions

G) wrote book, *Foreign Conspiracy against the Liberties of the United States;* inventor of the telegraph

H) consecrated Bishop of Philadelphia in 1852

I) troubled girl who wrote best seller in which lies were spread about the Church

J) Irish Bishop of New York who continually fought for Catholics against Nativism

K) secretive society dedicated to anti-Catholic activities

L) alleged father of Maria Monk's baby

M) convent in which Maria Monk claimed she lived for five years

**Mini-Essay Question:** (Extra credit—4 points.) List the specific condemnations of the Americanist Heresy that Pope Leo XIII stated in *Testem Benevolentiae* ("On True and False Americanism in Religion").

**Personal Opinion:** Name an important or interesting fact that you learned in this chapter. How could this fact affect your life?

**Supplemental Reading**

Ann Ball. *Modern Saints—Their Lives and Faces*, Book One, pp. 22-28 (St. John Neumann). TAN.

Fr. Robert J. Fox. *Saints and Heroes Speak*, Vol. 2, pp. 101-110 (St. John Neumann). Fatima Family Apostolate.

# 15 THE COMING OF THE CIVIL WAR

Text Pages 197-212

**Perfect Score: 100** **Score:** ______________
(Each Question is worth 2 points.)

## Completion

**Directions:** Complete and make each statement true and accurate by writing one or more words on each blank line.

1. Even though slaves were considered property by Southerners, the Constitution allowed the Southern states to count them when determining its number of representatives in Congress, each slave being worth ______________ of a white man.

2. As a result of the Missouri Compromise of 1820, two states were admitted to the union; Missouri would be a slave state, but ______________ would be free.

3. The Abolitionist Movement's earliest leaders were the ______________ of Philadelphia.

4. ______________ abolitionists such as Adams and Weld could foresee that society would be greatly disrupted if a total end to slavery were sought immediately.

5. The state of ______________ was delayed in its annexation to the United States until 1845 by abolitionists who knew that it would be made a slave state.

6. During the "Great Debate," in which Henry Clay proposed that California be admitted to the U.S. as a free state and the territory annexed after the Mexican War be organized without restriction on slavery, William H. Seward opposed the compromise, arguing that God's law is higher than the ______________ .

7. The Compromise of 1850 adopted Henry Clay's proposals as well as tightened fugitive slave laws to please the South. To appease the North, slavery was abolished in the ______________ .

8. The Republican Party in 1854 was made up of three groups who wanted to end slavery: Free-Soil Party members, anti-slavery Democrats and ______________________. The Republican Party wanted a repeal of the Fugitive Slave Laws and the Kansas-Nebraska Act as well as the end of slavery in the District of Columbia.

9. Colonel Robert E. Lee recaptured the federal ______________________ and armory at Harper's Ferry, which John Brown and his followers had seized on October 16, 1858.

10. The states of North Carolina, Arkansas, Virginia and Tennessee seceded from the Union after federal Fort ______________________ outside of Charleston, South Carolina was attacked in April of 1861.

11. While Colonel Robert E. Lee from Virginia did not condone slavery and saw secession of states as a great tragedy, he was loyal to the South and thus refused Winfield Scott's offer of field command of the ______________________ armies.

12. After Robert E. Lee's refusal, General Irvin ______________________ was appointed to command the Army of the Potomac.

13. Scott recommended a plan of blockading the Southern coastline and slowly starving the South; this plan was nicknamed the "______________________ Strategy."

14. In his inaugural address, Lincoln said, "I hold that . . . the union of the states is ______________________."

## Multiple Choice

**Directions:** After each statement below, there is a set of words or phrases. Circle the letter next to the one word or phrase that best completes the sentence.

1. Characteristics of the Southern states just prior to the Civil War included all of the following except:
   a) upheld the power of federal government over state government
   b) kept to a farm-centered way of life
   c) upheld hierarchical authority in families and communities
   d) honored home, family and land more than the Union
   e) none of the above; they *all* describe the Southern states

2. In 1819, with the number of free and slave states equal at eleven each, the application by one territory for statehood caused tremendous debate in Congress because its legal status would upset the balance and raise the question of the legal status of the rest of the Louisiana Purchase territory. This state was:
   a) Texas
   b) Kansas
   c) Missouri
   d) Louisiana
   e) none of the above

3. The first abolitionist congressional leader, who wrote that slavery is "a great and foul stain upon the North American Union" and who introduced petitions in Congress to end slavery, was:
   a) Henry Clay
   b) John Quincy Adams
   c) William H. Seward
   d) Abraham Lincoln
   e) Charles Sumner

4. The legislation passed by Southern congressmen which required the return of runaway slaves was known as the:
   a) Underground Railroad
   b) Gag Rule
   c) compromise of slaves
   d) Fugitive Slave Laws
   e) Compromise of 1850

5. "The Address of the Southern Delegates" was delivered in 1849 by this spokesman for 69 Southerners in Congress; he accused the North of aggression against the South by prohibiting slave owners from taking their "property" into the new territories:
   a) John C. Calhoun
   b) Henry Clay
   c) William Lloyd Garrison
   d) Theodore Weld
   e) none of the above

6. The case of Dred Scott v. Sanford involved which critical issue(s):
   a) whether Scott was a citizen of Missouri, thus entitled to sue
   b) the constitutionality of the Missouri Compromise
   c) whether Scott's temporary stay in Wisconsin (free territory) gave him a title to freedom
   d) a and c only
   e) a, b and c

7. The Illinois Republican who made a speech in 1858 declaring that "a house divided against itself cannot stand" was:
   a) Henry Clay
   b) John Quincy Adams
   c) William H. Seward
   d) Abraham Lincoln
   e) Charles Sumner

8. The first state to secede from the Union (on December 20, 1860) was:
   a) Mississippi
   b) Florida
   c) South Carolina
   d) Alabama
   e) Georgia

9. The states that seceded from the U.S. beginning in 1860 formed the Confederate States of America. All of the following were in the Confederacy except:
   a) Texas
   b) Florida
   c) Alabama
   d) Georgia
   e) Missouri

10. The reasons the South won at First Manassas (First Battle of Bull Run) included:
    a) the sightseers from Washington deliberately sabotaging a bridge
    b) General Johnston's men marching to location to help
    c) Thomas "Stonewall" Jackson and Virginians making a brave stand
    d) a and b only
    e) b and c only

## True/False

**Directions:** Circle the letter T if the statement is true or F if the statement is false.

1. T F The Christian system of government during the Middle Ages included both a strong central authority and strong local authorities.

2. T F The Industrial Revolution was centered in the North.

3. T F The Great Revival was a Protestant movement in the 1830s that encouraged men to do good by improving society through social reforms. This reform was inspired as a reaction to the laxity and sloth of Calvinism.

4. T F The Underground Railroad was a secret train by which fugitive slaves were able to escape to the North.

5. T F The press in the United States was very powerful at the time of the Abolitionist Movement and Underground Railway, when Northern newspapers inflamed the growing discontent of the abolitionists.

6. T F The Gag Rule was designed to stop Congress from acting on anti-slavery petitions. Northerners felt this was an obstruction of their free speech.

7. T F Senator William H. Seward proposed popular sovereignty as a solution to the question of slavery, changing the slavery debate from a moral issue into a problem solvable by a majority vote.

8. T F The Kansas-Nebraska Act, which passed in 1854, gave Americans the needed push to face the unknown and slowly and gradually settle the new territories.

9. T F An effect of the Kansas-Nebraska Act was that the different anti-slavery groups joined together.

10. T F Senator Sumner's speech entitled "The Crime against Kansas" (1856) attacked proposed legislation to make Kansas a free state.

11. T F Preston Brooks' physical attack on Senator Butler was cited as evidence that the North would never listen to reason.

12. T F In the Court ruling against Dred Scott, the Court declared an act of Congress, the Missouri Compromise, to be unconstitutional and decreed that black people were property, not persons.

13. T F In the presidential election of 1860, Lincoln received a majority of the popular vote in both North and South, thus winning the election.

## Matching

**Directions:** This list is made up of names of persons, groups, places and things. Each one corresponds to one of the lettered phrases below. In each blank, write the letter of the phrase that correctly identifies that person, group, place or thing.

1. ___ James Buchanan
2. ___ Harriet Beecher Stowe
3. ___ Theodore Weld
4. ___ William Lloyd Garrison
5. ___ John C. Calhoun
6. ___ William H. Seward
7. ___ Stephen Douglas
8. ___ Henry Ward Beecher
9. ___ John Brown
10. ___ John W. Geary
11. ___ Jefferson Davis
12. ___ Nathaniel Lyons
13. ___ Winfield Scott

A) Illinois Senator; the "Little Giant"; proposed popular sovereignty
B) Captain appointed by Lincoln to stop Missouri from seceding from Union
C) first leader of abolitionists; founded New England anti-slavery societies
D) Democratic president; supported popular sovereignty and noninterference with slavery in the states
E) Protestant abolitionist minister; thought Kansas should be taken by rifle if necessary
F) Mississippi Congressman elected President of the Confederacy
G) radical abolitionist leader; called Constitution "a Covenant with death"
H) unbalanced abolitionist who murdered pro-slavery men in retaliation; seized federal arsenal at Harper's Ferry
I) argued in "Great Debate" that God's law is higher than the Constitution
J) Commander-in-Chief of the Union armies; predicted war would last three years
K) wrote *Uncle Tom's Cabin* in 1852; this book further inflamed Northern sentiment against the South
L) Governor who brought order to "Bleeding Kansas"
M) South Carolina Senator who saw slavery as a positive good

**Mini-Essay Question:** (Extra credit—4 points.) With the coming of secession and war, while the slavery issue was the most important issue to both the North and the South, both sides had other goals as well. Give two additional goals of each side.

**Personal Opinion:** Name an important or interesting fact that you learned in this chapter. How could this fact affect your life?

# 16 THE CIVIL WAR

Text Pages 214-232

**Perfect Score: 100** **Score:** ________________
(Each Question is worth 2 points.)

## Completion

**Directions:** Complete and make each statement true and accurate by writing one or more words on each blank line.

1. The capital of the ______________________, and therefore a key strategic point for the Union generals to capture, was Richmond, Virginia.
2. General Robert E. Lee, commander of the Army of Northern Virginia, devised a plan that stopped McClellan's projected invasion of ______________________.
3. Because most of the violence and fighting had taken place in the ______________________ Valley up to mid-June of 1863, this valley was devastated. Lee decided to take the fighting north, and he proceeded to move his army to Pennsylvania.
4. Because of Generals Ewell and ______________________, the major blow Lee had wanted to deliver at Cemetery Ridge did not take place.
5. The battle fought up the steep rocky hill known as Little ______________________ Top between Hood and Warren resulted in the Union preventing a Confederate effort to flank the Army of the Potomac.
6. When James Longstreet failed to ensure a steady ______________________ supply at Gettysburg, the Confederacy suffered severe casualties and the South lost a critical battle that it desperately needed to win.
7. General ______________________ was not known for his neat appearance; he was known for his heavy drinking.
8. The confused instructions that Major Bond delivered to General Wood—that he was to close up on Reynolds as fast as possible and support him—are known as the "muddled orders of ______________________."

9. The battle in May of 1864 between Generals Lee and Grant among the mass of trees known as the ______________________ was fought amidst smoke; the battle resulted in the loss of twice as many Union soldiers as Confederate soldiers.

10. After Petersburg was taken by the Union, General Robert E. Lee took his troops to Amelia Courthouse, then Danville, and after failing to find desperately needed supplies, he marched on to ______________________ Station. Learning that all lines were cut off by the Union Army, he decided to surrender.

11. When General Lee met with General Grant at the home of Major Wilmer ______________________ to sign the surrender document on April 9, 1864, he was in full dress uniform with gold sword.

12. General Robert E. Lee had an outstanding record throughout the Civil War despite the constant lack of men and supplies; he repulsed four major offensives and decisively won ______________________ of the ten major battles fought between 1862-1864, losing only Gettysburg.

13. Abraham Lincoln had begun his presidency determined to do everything necessary to restore the Union and guarantee the survival of ______________________ government.

14. Lincoln violated the Constitution when he denied the right of ______________________ without Congress's consent.

## Multiple Choice

**Directions:** After each statement below, there is a set of words or phrases. Circle the letter next to the one word or phrase that best completes the sentence.

1. Union Admiral David Faragut captured the Confederacy's largest and wealthiest city, which was its main port. This city was:
   a) Richmond
   b) Charleston
   c) Vicksburg
   d) New Orleans
   e) none of the above

2. Abraham Lincoln issued the Emancipation Proclamation following this battle, which appeared to be a Union victory but was actually a draw:
   a) Antietam
   b) Gettysburg
   c) Vicksburg
   d) Second Manassas
   e) Chickamauga

3. Northerners became dissatisfied with Abraham Lincoln because:
   a) they considered the Emancipation Proclamation too harsh/too lenient
   b) he revoked the right of *habeas corpus*
   c) he ordered the draft
   d) a and b only
   e) a, b and c

4. The Union General who took Chattanooga, giving the Northern armies a strategic advantage and ability to split the South, was:
   a) Grant
   b) Hooker
   c) Sheridan
   d) Thomas
   e) Burnside

5. The Confederacy under Robert E. Lee suffered from all except:
   a) a sea blockade
   b) the loss of Vicksburg
   c) inability to manufacture/distribute supplies
   d) poor leadership
   e) being outnumbered

6. The 16-hour battle fought at Spotsylvania became known as:
   a) the Wilderness
   b) Bloody Angle
   c) Appomattox Station
   d) the "absolute masterpiece"
   e) Antietam

7. Confederate General Johnston was defeated a number of times by this Union General who destroyed everything in his path through the state of Georgia. He was:
   a) Grant
   b) Sherman
   c) Thomas
   d) McClellan
   e) Wood

8. With the capture of this city by General Thomas, the Confederate line was broken and the war in the West ended:
   a) Chattanooga
   b) Chickamauga
   c) Spotsylvania
   d) Nashville
   e) none of the above

9. During Abraham Lincoln's re-election, he carried every state with the exception of:
   a) Kentucky
   b) New Jersey
   c) Delaware
   d) all of the above

10. Abraham Lincoln's shortcomings included:
   a) American Messianism
   b) violation of civil liberties
   c) inability to forgive the South
   d) a and b only
   e) a, b and c

## True/False

**Directions:** Circle the letter T if the statement is true or F if the statement is false.

1. T F Lincoln supported Grant against the Northern newspapers and Congressmen because even though the casualties were heavy, Lincoln appreciated the fact that Grant was aggressive and took chances.

2. T F When General Hooker tried to get Burnside fired, his plan backfired, as Lincoln removed Hooker and replaced him with Burnside.

3. T F The "absolute masterpiece" at the Battle of Chancellorsville, planned by Hooker, turned out to be a brilliant strategic triumph for General Robert E. Lee.

4. T F The draft that Lincoln ordered led to the kidnapping of innocent people, who were then forced to serve in the Army.

5. T F Lee refused to attack civilians or let Confederate soldiers destroy Northern farms and homes.

6. T F When Grant besieged Vicksburg, his men were not able to maintain their siege against the Southerners inside.

7. T F After his devastating defeat at the Wilderness, where 100 men were killed every minute, Grant, demoralized by General Lee, led his men back to Washington to regroup.

8. T F At Bloody Angle, Grant used a strategy of continuing to wear down the Southern forces at the cost of many Union soldiers, and his strategy proved effective.

9. T F The Confederate troops received repeating carbines in June of 1864 that shot twice as fast as before, making General Grant believe their army was bigger.

10. T F The 15th amendment to the Constitution, which abolished slavery, was enacted in Congress after Lincoln's re-election as President.

11. T F After General Lee surrendered in April of 1865, Johnston surrendered to Sherman; then, in May, the last Confederate forces surrendered.

12. T F John Wilkes Booth assassinated President Lincoln shortly after the war ended.

13. T F Abraham Lincoln was able to lead a divided nation despite opposition from the press, the Congress, the Cabinet and the state governments.

## Matching

**Directions:** This list is made up of names of persons, groups, places and things. Each one corresponds to one of the lettered phrases below. In each blank, write the letter of the phrase that correctly identifies that person, group, place or thing.

1. ___ George McClellan
2. ___ Charles Francis Adams
3. ___ Edwin M. Stanton
4. ___ Henry Halleck
5. ___ John Pope
6. ___ Joseph Hooker
7. ___ George Meade
8. ___ James Longstreet
9. ___ General Ewell
10. ___ General Pickett
11. ___ George Thomas
12. ___ Philip Sheridan
13. ___ Jeb Stewart

A) General-in-Chief who replaced McClellan
B) led elite, courageous, Virginia division into the Union fire at Gettysburg
C) "Young Napoleon"; replaced McDowell as commander of the Army of the Potomac and Scott as General-in-Chief
D) replaced Stonewall Jackson as Lee's second-in-command
E) Union General known as the Rock of Chickamauga; took Chattanooga
F) Lincoln's competent Secretary of War who thoroughly equipped the northern army
G) Confederate General; took Culp's Hill but did not move to take Cemetery Ridge at Gettysburg
H) Northern cavalry commander who cut off Southern supply lines
I) persuaded British government not to go beyond their neutrality with the South
J) General who devised the plan known as an "absolute masterpiece"
K) best scout of Confederacy; killed while heading off Sheridan's troops on their way to Richmond
L) Lincoln's General in command of the Armies of Virginia after McClellan; obsessed with defeating Jackson
M) General who sent Warren up Little Round Top

**Mini-Essay Question:** (Extra credit—4 points.) Tell what the Emancipation Proclamation was as well as America's reaction to the Proclamation.

**Personal Opinion:** Name an important or interesting fact that you learned in this chapter. How could this fact affect your life?

**Supplemental Reading**

*The Emancipation Proclamation.*

# 17 TRADITIONALISTS IN LATIN AMERICA

Text Pages 234-246

**Perfect Score: 100** **Score:** ________________

(Each Question is worth 2 points.)

## Completion

**Directions:** Complete and make each statement true and accurate by writing one or more words on each blank line.

1. For 40 years after the overthrow of Iturbide (1823-1863), Mexico was engaged in ______________________ war, with traditionalists fighting liberals for control of the government. An example of the disorder and chaos was the fact that there were 30 presidents in 30 years.

2. After overthrowing Santa Anna in 1854, Benito Juarez was able to fight the traditionalist rebellion only with help from the ______________________, which supplied Juarez with weapons and money, enabling him to win the civil war.

3. The Laws of the ______________________, which Juarez promulgated in 1859, confiscated Church land, money and objects.

4. Mexico's debt to foreign countries continued to mount under Juarez until he declared a ______________________ on all foreign debts in 1861, thereby alienating the European countries who had assisted him. It was then that these countries began to consider getting a European prince to rule Mexico.

5 ______________________, who was intelligent, creative and committed, dominated the decisions in Mexican government during the reign of her husband, Emperor Maximilian I.

6. The U.S. Secretary of State refused to receive Maximilian's ambassador, referring to him as a "______________________."

7. Napoleon III had promised Maximilian three years of French army protection, but he went back on his promise within two years, stating that the French armies could stay only if all Mexican ______________________ were turned over to France. With the debt that Mexico owed to several other countries, this was impossible.

8. As President of Mexico, General Porfirio Diaz did not let any one group gain too much power; he balanced landowners and peasants, laborers and ______________________, soldiers and politicians.

9. Diaz's financial dependence upon the United States and other countries, and his giving of Indian community lands to wealthy landlords called ______________________, were two of his biggest mistakes. This resulted in foreign investors and a few thousand wealthy families owning Mexico.

10. When asked when he had last gone to ______________________, Gabriel Garcia Moreno faced the realization that if one truly believes in the doctrines of Catholicism, he should live a totally Catholic life. This question from a non-Catholic friend changed his life.

11. Following his conversion to a deeper commitment to Christ, Moreno realized he must try to ______________________ society.

12. During Moreno's service to Ecuador, his newspaper publishing resulted in him having to flee the country twice to save his life from liberals who hated him. The first time he fled to Paris, the second time to ______________________.

13. One of the things Moreno did as President of Ecuador was to sign a ______________________ with the Vatican in 1863, eliminating government interference in the Church.

14. Moreno managed his internal affairs with great prudence so that Ecuador had a ______________________ budget. He achieved this without raising taxes or borrowing money.

## Multiple Choice

**Directions:** After each statement below, there is a set of words or phrases. Circle the letter next to the one word or phrase that best completes the sentence.

1. The government of Benito Juarez, who took over Mexico City in 1861, was heavily indebted to all of the following European countries except:
   a) England
   b) Italy
   c) France
   d) Spain

2. After two visits to Napoleon III failed to persuade him to continue financial and military support of Mexico, Carlota telegrammed Max with the message:
   a) Viva Independencia
   b) Todo es inutil
   c) Viva Mexico
   d) Todo es desperado
   e) none of the above

3. When Carlota knew that her mission to Paris was a failure, she became insane with paranoia. The Hapsburgs brought her back to Trieste, Italy until her sister-in-law later brought her home to a castle where she lived until her death in 1927 in the country of:
   a) Italy
   b) Austria
   c) Belgium
   d) Portugal
   e) Spain

4. Under the Diaz government, anti-Catholic laws in Mexico were not enforced, so that by 1890 the Church experienced:
   a) reforms of convents and monasteries
   b) restoration of all Church property
   c) Catholic schools in operation again
   d) a and c only
   e) a, b and c

5. While in Congress, Moreno's primary efforts were concentrated on two specific issues. One of these issues was:
   a) curbing Freemasonic activities
   b) funding roads
   c) reforming hospitals
   d) curbing crime
   e) building Catholic schools

6. The Battle at Guayaquil was won by Moreno's men on September 24, 1859, on the Feast that would in the future be observed each year by the army and government of Ecuador:
   a) Our Lady of Perpetual Help
   b) Our Lady of Good Remedy
   c) Our Lady of Good Success
   d) Our Lady of Ransom
   e) Our Lady of Good Counsel

7. Under the guidance and protection of the Patroness of Ecuador, Moreno achieved all of the following except:
   a) cutting expenditures and balancing the budget
   b) restoring discipline to the army
   c) constructing new roads for commerce
   d) entrusting the hospitals to the Sisters of Mercy
   e) establishing Catholic schools

8. Moreno believed in eliciting assistance from the congregations in the Church. He sent the following throughout Ecuador to bring fallen-away Catholics back to the Church:
   a) Redemptorists
   b) Jesuits
   c) Sisters of Charity
   d) Franciscans

9. Moreno's motto was:
   a) God and country
   b) Viva Independencia
   c) Pan o palo
   d) Nothing by force, everything by law and reason
   e) God never dies. God is, that is enough

10. After the six dictators who followed Moreno's death, Ecuador saw 50 years of constant changes in the presidency. From 1895, with the new liberal government, to 1945, Ecuador had the following number of presidents:
    a) 10
    b) 20
    c) 30
    d) 40
    e) none of the above

## True/False

**Directions:** Circle the letter T if the statement is true or F if the statement is false.

1. T F After the rebellion against Spain, most of the ordinary people in Latin America were true to their Catholic Faith, but all the men of the wealthier classes were only interested in using their country to gain more wealth and power for themselves.

2. T F Since Benito Juarez was Indian himself, he made sure the Indians who lived on Church lands were well taken care of.

3. T F Although Abraham Lincoln supported the reign of Emperor Maximilian I in Mexico, he could not provide help because of the Civil War in the U.S.

4. T F By the end of Carlota's stressful mission to Paris in 1866, she had become insane.

5. T F Benito Juarez executed Maximilian, Miramón and Mejía on the Hill of the Bells on June 19, 1867, each of them carrying a crucifix.

6. T F Benito Juarez's rule finally ended when he was assassinated in 1872.

7. T F The problem of bandits plagued both Diaz in Mexico and Moreno in Ecuador. Diaz gave the bandit chiefs a choice—five fingers in a handshake or five bullets.

8. T F While Moreno was exiled in Peru, a traditionalist rebellion broke out in Quito and its leaders begged Moreno to command the patriot troops.

9. T F When Moreno was captured and condemned to die, he escaped when members of the traditionalist army came at night and overtook the guard.

10. T F Under Moreno as president, the people of Ecuador adopted a new constitution that proclaimed Catholicism the official religion of Ecuador.

11. T F Despite all of his other achievements, because of bandits, Moreno was never quite able to get crime under control; more prisons were needed.

12. T F As his presidential term was coming to an end, Moreno was assassinated when he went to Santiago, Chile to arrange a treaty.

13. T F After Moreno's death, Ecuador suffered from civil war, lawlessness, economic depression and dictators.

## Matching

**Directions:** This list is made up of names of persons, groups, places and things. Each one corresponds to one of the lettered phrases below. In each blank, write the letter of the phrase that correctly identifies that person, group, place or thing.

1. ___ Rafael Carrera
2. ___ Miguel Antonio Caro
3. ___ Maximilian von Hapsburg
4. ___ Princess Charlotte of Belgium
5. ___ José d'Estrada and José Hidalgo
6. ___ Eugenie
7. ___ Benito Juarez
8. ___ Almonte

9. ___ Mejía and Miramón

10. ___ Miguel Lopez

11. ___ Lerdo

12. ___ Porfirio Diaz

13. ___ Gabriel Garcia Moreno

A) published *The Nation* to defend Catholicism; critical of government in Ecuador

B) General who convened a national assembly in Mexico to ask Maximilian to accept the throne

C) Mexican leaders who conceived idea of a Catholic monarchy with a European prince for Mexico

D) traditionalist intellectual who stabilized and guided Columbia from 1843-1909

E) traditionalist Mexican generals who assisted Maximilian; were executed with him

F) liberal ruler of Mexico from 1854-63 (overthrew Santa Anna) and 1867-72 (overthrew Maximilian)

G) brother of Franz Josef of Austria

H) Empress of France; wife of Napoleon III; urged him to bring a Catholic emperor to Mexico

I) officer who betrayed Maximilian for Juarez out of anger over not being made a general

J) General who took over Mexican government in 1876; first Mexican president to keep order

K) lieutenant; unpopular successor of Juarez; defeated by Porfirio Diaz

L) traditionalist Catholic Indian; governed Guatemala from 1838-65

M) became Empress of Mexico; collapsed into insanity

**Mini-Essay Question:** (Extra credit—4 points.) Explain how the U.S. and French governments contributed to the death of Emperor Maximilian I and the insanity of his wife.

**Personal Opinion:** Name an important or interesting fact that you learned in this chapter. How could this fact affect your life?

**Supplemental Reading**

Joan Haslip. *The Crown of Mexico: Maximilian and His Empress Carlota.*

# 18 THE UNITED STATES IN THE GILDED AGE

Text Pages 248-264

**Perfect Score: 100** **Score:** ________________

(Each Question is worth 2 points.)

## Completion

**Directions:** Complete and make each statement true and accurate by writing one or more words on each blank line.

1. President Andrew Johnson issued ______________________ Proclamations in May 1865 with the intention of restoring rights to Southerners who took an oath of support to the government. Johnson intended to follow up on the plans begun by Abraham Lincoln before his assassination.

2. The radical Republicans Theodore Stevens and Charles Sumner dominated the 39th Congress, refusing to accept Johnson's policies or admit ______________________ delegates to Congress.

3. The Civil Rights Act granted citizenship to blacks and civil rights to all persons born in the U.S., except ______________________ .

4. In order for Southern states to be readmitted to the Union, they had to ______________________ the Fourteenth Amendment.

5. Although Johnson was innocent, because he opposed the radical Republicans at every opportunity, the House of Representatives ______________________ Johnson. When the Senate voted to convict him, however, they lacked the needed two-thirds majority.

6. For 80 years, the solid South voted as a block for the ______________________ Party as a reaction against the Reconstruction policies promulgated by the Republicans.

7. In the Hayes administration, the main controversy involved how ______________________ would be supplied in the country, with various factions vying for their way.

8. The 1880 presidential election saw the issue of ______________________, appointing friends to political offices, versus civil service, making appointments based on merit.

9. The ______________________ Party was formed in 1892. Its agenda included an inflationary increase in the money supply and putting checks on the power of banks and big business.

10. The encyclical issued in 1891 by Pope Leo XIII, which reversed the decision of the Quebec Bishops, was titled, *Rerum Novarum* or "The Condition of the ______________________ Classes."

11. Almost all of the nurses who assisted the wounded and dying during the Civil War belonged to Elizabeth Ann Seton's Sisters of ______________________ .

12. A major problem that the French Bishop Lamy faced was trying to reform the immoral lives of the priests in the ______________________ territory.

13. The number of churches and chapels in Bishop Lamy's diocese increased dramatically under him, from 66 to ______________________ . He also established schools, colleges, a hospital, an orphanage, novitiate and seminary, accomplishing all of this before his retirement in 1885 at the age of 73.

14. When ______________________ was told that the U.S. Government had decided that only four of the 43 missions in the west would be Catholic, he replied that the Indians had not been consulted as to what religion they desired to belong to.

## Multiple Choice

**Directions:** After each statement below, there is a set of words or phrases. Circle the letter next to the one word or phrase that best completes the sentence.

1. The laws enacted in the South after the Civil War that forbade blacks from accessing city jobs were known as:
   a) Jim Crow Laws
   b) Black Codes
   c) Reconstruction Acts
   d) none of the above

2. The only Southern state to ratify the Fourteenth Amendment was:
   a) Kentucky
   b) Louisiana
   c) Mississippi
   d) Alabama
   e) Tennessee

3. In the 1876 Presidential election between Rutherford Hayes and Samuel Tilden, Republicans would not concede the election because they held that the electoral returns in three Southern states were in dispute. The three states in question included all except:
   a) Mississippi
   b) Florida
   c) Louisiana
   d) South Carolina

4. The laws enacted in the South that essentially segregated black people from places that white people frequented were called:
   a) Jim Crow Laws
   b) Black Codes
   c) Reconstruction Acts
   d) none of the above

5. The various solutions to the question of the money supply during the Hayes administration in 1876 included all of the following except:
   a) a gold standard
   b) unredeemable paper money
   c) a copper standard
   d) bimetallism

6. The labor union formed at the beginning of the labor union movement in 1878 to improve working conditions and wages was known as:
   a) Quebec Labor Union
   b) Knights of Labor
   c) Factory Labor Union
   d) American Federation of Labor
   e) American Labor Union

7. Bishop Lamy had a wide diocese in the territorial United States; it included the territory which has become all of the following states except:
   a) Utah
   b) Colorado
   c) Arizona
   d) New Mexico

8. Bishop Lamy accomplished a great deal in his diocese, including all of the following except:
   a) staffing a school with the Sisters of Loretto
   b) increasing the number of priests
   c) founding the Indian mission at Council Bluffs
   d) building a cathedral honoring St. Francis of Assisi

9. Because Father De Smet loved the Indians so much and they respected him in return, he was able to work with various Indian groups such as the Flatheads and Nez Perce, establishing missions and helping keep the peace in the following state(s):
   a) Iowa
   b) Oregon
   c) Wyoming
   d) Montana
   e) all of the above

10. Sister Blandina Segale ministered to the sick and taught children in this city:
   a) Toronto
   b) San Antonio
   c) St. Louis
   d) Denver
   e) none of the above

# True/False

**Directions:** Circle the letter T if the statement is true or F if the statement is false.

1. T F By April of 1866, every Southern state had conformed to the provisions of the Reconstruction Proclamation.

2. T F As a sign of good will in Reconstruction, all fourteen special cases of Southerners requiring a request for individual pardon were immediately granted by President Johnson.

3. T F The Ku Klux Klan was founded in 1866 with the intention of keeping blacks from voting and later to do them bodily harm.

4. T F After establishing the Freedman's Bureau, Congress gave it the power to try by military commission anyone accused of depriving freedmen of their rights.

5. T F The Thirteenth Amendment included Negroes in its definition of national citizenship and declared that no state could "deprive any person of life, liberty, or property, without due process of law, nor deny to any person within its jurisdiction the equal protection of the laws."

6. T F When the First Reconstruction Act failed to force the Southern states to establish new governments that would guarantee voting rights for black people, Congress gave the military governments the power to enroll voters and hold elections through the Supplementary Reconstruction Acts.

7. T F Grant lost to Horace Greeley in the presidential election of 1872 because even the Republicans were embarrassed by the corruption in Grant's administration.

8. T F Reconstruction ended when Hayes won the 1876 presidential election and made concessions to the Democrats, including the withdrawal of Federal troops from the South.

9. T F When the Republican Party split during the 1880 presidential election, the Halfbreeds supported Grant while the Stalwarts supported James Blaine of Maine.

10. T F The last third of the 19th century is known as the "Gilded Age" because the nation's wealth increased during this time and wealthy families built ornate, gilded mansions.

11. T F As a result of the Industrial Revolution, which came to America in the early 19th century, men moved from farms to cities, becoming financially dependent on businessmen and factory owners.

12. T F The Sherman Antitrust Act of 1890 put an end to the spread of monopolies.

13. T F Father De Smet proposed a policy to benefit the Indians that called for the gradual development of agricultural programs, and he assisted the Sioux and Cheyenne Indians in coming to treaty terms with the government.

# Matching

**Directions:** This list is made up of names of persons, groups, places and things. Each one corresponds to one of the lettered phrases below. In each blank, write the letter of the phrase that correctly identifies that person, group, place or thing.

1. ___ James G. Blaine
2. ___ scalawags
3. ___ carpetbaggers
4. ___ Edward Ross
5. ___ Samuel Tilden
6. ___ James Garfield
7. ___ Charles Guiteau
8. ___ John D. Rockefeller
9. ___ Terence Powderly
10. ___ James Gibbons
11. ___ Father Joseph Machebeuf
12. ___ Father Pierre-Jean De Smet
13. ___ George Armstrong Custer

A) shot and killed Garfield because he had wanted Arthur for the presidency
B) Vicar General to Bishop Lamy; first Bishop of Colorado
C) New York governor; Democratic opponent to Hayes in the 1876 presidential election
D) white southerners who approved of black voting rights and the Fourteenth Amendment
E) Jesuit priest; mediator between Indians and U.S. government
F) capitalist who formed the monopoly Standard Oil
G) lost support of New York in 1884 presidential campaign because of anti-Catholicism
H) widely respected Archbishop of Baltimore; reported labor conditions in America to Pope Leo XIII
I) compromise candidate in the 1880 presidential election between Blaine and Grant
J) first important leader of the Knights of Labor
K) northerners who came to the South to assist the military governments
L) General; Civil War veteran who attacked Indians in Second Sioux War
M) Kansas Senator who voted against conviction of Andrew Johnson at the sacrifice of his own career

**Mini-Essay Question**: (Extra credit—4 points.) Explain how the U.S. government's refusal to listen to Father De Smet's recommendations regarding the Indians led to tragedy for the Indians.

**Personal Opinion:** Name an important or interesting fact that you learned in this chapter. How could this fact affect your life?

**Supplemental Reading**

Fr. Laveille, S.J. *The Life of Father De Smet, S.J.—Apostle of the Rocky Mountains (1803-1873)*. TAN.

Regarding St. Anthony Mary Claret's ministry as Archbishop of Cuba:
Fr. Juan Echevarria. *The Miracles of St. Anthony Mary Claret*, pp. 143-198. TAN.

# 19 THE AGE OF THEODORE ROOSEVELT

Text Pages 266-280

**Perfect Score: 100** **Score:** ______________

(Each Question is worth 2 points.)

## Completion

**Directions:** Complete and make each statement true and accurate by writing one or more words on each blank line.

1. Although initially hostile to the purchase of Alaska, Americans were delighted in 1896 when gold was found in the ____________________ .
2. The Spanish ambassador expressed his opinion that President McKinley was weak in the " ____________________ Letter," which was stolen and published in William Randolph Hearst's *Journal* in February of 1898.
3. "Remember the ____________________ !" was the nation's cry when it believed that Spain had blown up the U.S. battleship in the Havana harbor in 1898.
4. When Upton Sinclair published his novel, *The* ____________________ , one of his primary purposes was to bring people into the socialist movement.
5. Theodore Roosevelt's two terms as President resulted in a significant move toward Big ____________________ , as people began more and more to believe that government had the solution for everything that ailed the country.
6. The great control that states acquired over what children were taught was inevitable with the passage of ____________________ school attendance laws in the 19th century.
7. The enormously influential Supreme Court Justice Oliver Wendell Holmes, Jr., did not advocate basing decisions firmly on moral principles, but instead stated that law corresponds with "what is understood to be ____________________ ."
8. At the time the U.S. was interested in building a canal across Central America, the proposed location, ____________________ , was a province of Columbia.

9. The U.S. pronouncement that the U.S. would become an international police power regarding the affairs of Latin America became known as the Roosevelt ______________________ to the Monroe Doctrine.

10. The first American citizen to be declared a Saint was ______________________ .

11. By 1888, the Sisters of St. Francis of Syracuse were ministering to the lepers on the island of ______________________ , where Father Damien had worked.

12. Xavier University, in the city of ______________________ , was founded by Kathryn Drexel to provide college education for blacks.

13. Kathryn Drexel, who founded the Sisters of the ______________________ , advocated the Sacred Heart devotion as an antidote to coldness in the world; she said, "The renewal which I seek and which we all seek is a work of love and can be accomplished by love alone."

14. The ______________________ missionaries, founded as the Catholic Foreign Mission Society of America by Thomas Price and Father James Anthony Walsh, sent missionaries to China.

## Multiple Choice

**Directions:** After each statement below, there is a set of words or phrases. Circle the letter next to the one word or phrase that best completes the sentence.

1. Hawaii was annexed to the United States on July 7, 1898, as a result of imperialist pressures, during the presidency of:
   a) Cleveland
   b) McKinley
   c) Roosevelt
   d) Taft
   e) none of the above

2. Because of the United States' aggressive action in the Spanish American War, Spain lost much of its territory in Central America. The treaty signed in 1898 saw Cuba gaining independence, while Spain ceded to the United States all of the following except:
   a) Puerto Rico
   b) Philippines
   c) Virgin Islands
   d) Guam

3. The Cuban constitutional convention held in 1900 adopted concessions mandated by the U.S., including authorization of the U.S. to intervene to preserve Cuban independence; also, Cuba was required to sell or lease lands for U.S. naval use. The amendment which embodied these concessions was named after the Connecticut Senator who developed it:
   a) Bryan
   b) Sherman
   c) Hepburn
   d) Platt
   e) none of the above

4. Theodore Roosevelt, always a man of action, accomplished many things during his presidency. All of the following can in some way be attributed to Roosevelt except:
   a) Congress passing the Amendment allowing federal income taxes
   b) Congress passing the Hepburn Act, granting more power to the Interstate Commerce Commission
   c) the U.S. gaining a ten-mile strip of land for the Panama Canal
   d) the Sherman Antitrust Act invoked against the Northern Securities Company

5. Roosevelt's popularity soared as many journalists focused on exposing corruption and scandals in business and government. These journalists were called:
   a) Mud Rangers
   b) Dirt throwers
   c) Mudslingers
   d) none of the above

6. The meat packing industry actually supported federal legislation regulating their industry because they hoped that the public would resume their consumption of meat. In 1906, the following law(s) was/were passed by the government in this regard:
   a) Meat Antitrust Act
   b) Pure Food and Drug Act
   c) Meat Inspection Act
   d) a and b only
   e) b and c only

7. The progressive movement initiated the following:
   a) initiative
   b) referendum
   c) direct primary
   d) recall
   e) all of the above

8. After Roosevelt had served two terms, William Howard Taft became president. But in the presidential election of 1912, Roosevelt attempted to resume the presidency at the cost of a friendship and the split of the Republican Party. When he could not get his way at the Republican convention, he formed his own party, the Progressive Party, that came to be known as the:
   a) Armageddon Party
   b) Bull Moose Party
   c) Armageddon Avengers
   d) Modernist Party
   e) none of the above

9. Mother Cabrini opened a school that functioned for two years, until 1894, when the anti-Catholic government forced the Sisters out. This happened in the country of:
   a) Nicaragua
   b) Columbia
   c) Peru
   d) Brazil
   e) Ecuador

10. After Kathryn Drexel founded Xavier University, she established schools in many cities, including:
   a) Santa Fe
   b) Harlem
   c) Chicago
   d) a and c only
   e) a, b and c

## True/False

**Directions:** Circle the letter T if the statement is true or F if the statement is false.

1. T F William Randolph Hearst and Joseph Pulitzer invented stories against Spain to sell their newspapers. This increased U.S. hostility toward Spain, which helped to pressure McKinley to declare war on Spain in 1898 when a U.S. battleship was blown up.

2. T F The Progressive Movement claimed to be modern in its approach to government; because the Progressives worked mainly at the national level, their changes were far-reaching.

3. T F The main goal of the Progressives was to give people more participation in the government, and their efforts led to the Seventeenth Amendment, which required the direct election of Senators.

4. T F Pragmatism is the belief that an idea must conform to the moral law in order for it to be deemed practical.

5. T F The Supreme Court cases *Lochner v. New York* (1905) and *Muller v. Oregon* (1908) showed how the Court always upholds its decisions, never contradicting itself.

6. T F Theodore Roosevelt's motto was, "Speak firmly and carry a big stick."

7. T F In 1903, the U.S. prevented Colombian troops from landing in Panama and recognized the independence of the Republic of Panama.

8. T F When Roosevelt mediated the settlement for the Russo-Japanese War, he helped to establish the U.S. as a major world force.

9. T F Taft's most significant act as president was getting Congress to pass the Sixteenth Amendment, which permitted taxes on all imported goods.

10. T F On October 28, 1886, President Cleveland dedicated the Statue of Liberty, a gift from Italy to the U.S.

11. T F Mother Cabrini came to the U.S. from Italy and founded many schools for black and Indian children in the New York City area, including the school for Indians where she is buried.

12. T F Mother Marianne Cope of the Sisters of St. Francis of Syracuse ministered to the lepers in Hawaii. Her Sisters never contracted leprosy.

13. T F When Rose Lathrop's friend died of cancer, she volunteered at a cancer hospital and then purchased a home for poor cancer victims. These experiences eventually lead to the founding of the Hawthorne Dominicans.

## Matching

**Directions:** This list is made up of names of persons, groups, places and things. Each one corresponds to one of the lettered phrases below. In each blank, write the letter of the phrase that correctly identifies that person, group, place or thing.

1. ___ Seward
2. ___ Sanford B. Dole
3. ___ John L. Stevens
4. ___ José Martí
5. ___ Valeriano Weyler
6. ___ Theodore Roosevelt
7. ___ Dr. Leonard Wood
8. ___ William Jennings Bryan
9. ___ Grove Johnson

10. ___ Oliver Wendell Holmes, Jr.

11. ___ William Howard Taft

12. ___ Woodrow Wilson

13. ___ James E. Walsh

A) military governor of Cuba after Spanish-American War; prepared Cubans to resume government of their island

B) judge appointed by Roosevelt to the U.S. Supreme Court in 1901; retired in 1932

C) U.S. ambassador to Hawaii; ordered U.S. Marines to occupy Hawaii and proclaimed it a U.S. protectorate

D) Secretary of State in 1866; purchased Alaska from Russia ($7,200,000)

E) Democratic candidate in the 1900 presidential election; denounced unrestricted capitalism

F) General in Cuba whose inhumane treatment of people earned him the name "The Butcher"

G) led Americans to overthrow Queen Liliuokalani; was proclaimed President of Hawaii for a short time

H) became U.S. president in 1908; urged Congress to permit federal income taxes

I) Maryknoll missionary; Bishop in China; spent years in Communist prison camp

J) Secretary of the Navy during Spanish-American War; Vice President to McKinley from 1900-1901; became President in 1901; formed Rough Riders

K) president in 1912 due to split of Republican Party; first Democratic president since Cleveland

L) poet and revolutionary; led Cuban rebels against Spain in 1895

M) California Republican who said, "The voice of the people is not the voice of God."

**Mini-Essay Question:** (Extra credit—4 points.) Describe Oliver Wendell Holmes, Jr.'s influence on the judicial system in the United States.

**Personal Opinion:** Name an important or interesting fact that you learned in this chapter. How could this fact affect your life?

**Supplemental Reading**

Ann Ball. *Modern Saints—Their Lives and Faces*, Book One, pp. 111-120 (Fr. Damien of Molokai); pp. 247-253 (St. Frances Cabrini); pp. 280-289 (Rose Hawthorne Lathrop); Book Two, pp. 287-293 (Mother Marianne of Molokai); pp. 456-466 (Katherine Drexel). TAN.

Fr. Robert J. Fox. *Saints and Heroes Speak*, Vol. 4, pp. 94-99 (Bishop James E. Walsh). Fatima Family Apostolate.

# 20 WOODROW WILSON AND THE FIRST WORLD WAR

Text Pages 282-298

**Perfect Score: 100** **Score:** ________________
(Each Question is worth 2 points.)

## Completion

**Directions:** Complete and make each statement true and accurate by writing one or more words on each blank line.

1. Before becoming President of the United States, Woodrow Wilson was President of ______________________ University.
2. The principle of Pragmatism leads to a rejection of absolute moral values. Wilson embraced pragmatism with this statement in 1907: "Liberty fixed in ______________________ law would be no liberty at all. Government . . . must change alike in its objects and its practices."
3. Wilson's "New ______________________ " platform called for stricter regulation of business, government control of the money supply in the U.S., and an income tax to reduce the amount of money in the hands of the wealthy.
4. At the time Wilson began reforming the banking system, the amount of government ______________________ that were sold determined how much money was available for loans.
5. With 12 ______________________ banks being set up under the umbrella of the Federal Reserve Board, the Federal Reserve banks were able to serve as a central banking institution.
6. Because Hughes criticized Wilson's demand for increased power in government, the Republicans came to be known from 1916 on as the ______________________ party, while the Democrats became the liberal party.
7. Wilson's first term as President focused on domestic affairs dealing with banking, social welfare and increasing government's power, while in his second term he moved into ______________________ affairs—with disastrous results for Europe.
8. In his speech calling for a declaration of war, Wilson told Congress that the United States was fighting "to make the world safe for ______________________ ."

9. When the Czar of Russia abdicated, ______________________ moved into power and set up a provisional government—to the praise of Wilson, who saw this turn of events as freedom for the Russian people.

10. Wilson's ______________________ Points, issued January 8, 1918, were the result of his opinions and philosophy of democracy as the only worthy form of government. These were used as the basis for peace negotiations and brought Wilson into conflict with Emperor Charles of Austria-Hungary.

11. Emperor Charles Hapsburg appealed to Wilson and reasoned that the people affected by Italy's territorial claims really wanted to be ruled by ______________________. Wilson flatly refused to acknowledge that a leader who was not elected could be the rightful ruler of any country.

12. The ______________________ Peace Conference underway in January 1919 saw Wilson, Clemenceau and Lloyd-George carrying out agendas of their own. The two European leaders devised punishments against Germany, while Wilson created countries in Europe without regard to the history of the peoples involved or to possible future problems.

13. Wilson's Messianism reached such heights that he actually made the statement that his League of Nations would accomplish the brotherhood of mankind where ______________________ had failed.

14. Because of Wilson's manipulation under the guise of "self-determination," the small countries previously ruled by Austria-Hungary were no longer protected and became victims of dictatorship, first Nazi and then ______________________.

## Multiple Choice

**Directions:** After each statement below, there is a set of words or phrases. Circle the letter next to the one word or phrase that best completes the sentence.

1. Woodrow Wilson wrote a book that detailed his governmental philosophy of power and strict accountability. It was published in 1885 and was titled:
   a) *Accountable Government*
   b) *Representative Government*
   c) *Congressional Government*
   d) *Electoral Government*

2. The principles advocated in Wilson's book included all of the following except:
    a) problems solved by elections
    b) pragmatism and rejection of absolute moral values
    c) individualism—the individual is more important than society
    d) power concentrated in the hands of government leaders

3. In order to gain more power, Wilson tried to gain the support of the following:
    a) Republican Party
    b) Democratic Party
    c) American public
    d) a and c only
    e) b and c only

4. In order to give government more power to break up big business, Wilson brought about the enactment of the following:
    a) Clayton Antitrust Act
    b) Underwood-Simmons Act
    c) Federal Farm Loan Act
    d) all of the above

5. The social welfare legislation enacted by Wilson, giving the federal government power that had henceforth been in the states, included all except:
    a) Underwood-Simmons Act
    b) Federal Farm Loan Act
    c) Adamson Act
    d) Child Labor Act

6. Despite the initial belief of the Allies of World War I that they could win the war in a few months, the war lasted four years (1914-1918) and took the lives of many of Europe's young men. Included among the Allied Forces was/were:
    a) Great Britain
    b) France
    c) Serbia
    d) a and b only
    e) a, b and c

7. Wilson kept the U.S. out of the war for almost two years after the Germans torpedoed this British passenger liner:
    a) Laconia
    b) Lusitania
    c) English Leisure Time
    d) none of the above

8. The Zimmerman Telegram was a code message in which the German Foreign Secretary tried to form an alliance with Mexico against the U.S. by promising Mexico all of the following except:
   a) New Mexico
   b) California
   c) Texas
   d) Arizona

9. The Armistice ending World War I was signed on November 11 of:
   a) 1916
   b) 1917
   c) 1918
   d) 1919

10. The leader at the Versailles Peace Conference who was wary of the long-term danger that could result from harsh punishment of the Germans and agreed that revisions should be made to the Treaty, but who went along with the punishments because his people wanted the Germans punished and because he wanted to stay in office, was:
   a) Wilson
   b) Lloyd-George
   c) Clemenceau
   d) none of the above

## True/False

**Directions:** Circle the letter T if the statement is true or F if the statement is false.

1. T F Wilson believed that there is nothing private in America, that everything belongs to the united energy of the nation.

2. T F Wilson believed and stated that, in a democracy, governmental power should be shared among as many representatives of the people as possible; thus, he worked hard to increase the power of the legislative branch of the federal government.

3. T F Wilson did not agree with punishing one's political enemies or rewarding political friends.

4. T F Wilson was able to get all of the major planks in his New Freedom platform enacted during one long session of Congress.

5. T F Because Wilson drove Congress as it had never been driven before, and because he had a tremendous ability to appeal to the people, Wilson is largely responsible for making the President the most powerful man in America.

6. T F Since Louis Brandeis was socialistic and relativistic, none of the Democrats on the Senate Judiciary Committee was opposed to him as Wilson's appointment to the Supreme Court.

7. T F Wilson used the slogan, "He kept us out of war" during his 1916 re-election campaign. Conversely, most of the Republican leaders at that time supported building up the military and entering the European war.

8. T F The two events that persuaded Wilson to enter the war were the Zimmerman Telegram and the sinking of the Lusitania.

9. T F Lenin and the Communists were able to take over Russia partly because Wilson and the other Allies virtually forced Kerensky to continue Russia's part in the war, leaving the country devastated.

10. T F Pope Pius X begged the warring governments to try to find a peaceful solution at the conference table.

11. T F When Wilson proceeded to redraw the map of Europe, putting into effect his plan of "self-determination," he united Czechs and Slovaks in the new country of Czechoslovakia, and he united Croatians, Serbians, Slovenes and Montenegrins in the new country of Yugoslavia because they shared the same religion and historical backgrounds.

12. T F When the Christian Ukranians expressed their desire to be free from the government of Russia because it was atheistic and Communist, Wilson told them to put their trust in God.

13. T F The Versailles Treaty was defeated in Congress, and America concluded a separate treaty.

## Matching

**Directions:** This list is made up of names of persons, groups, places and things. Each one corresponds to one of the lettered phrases below. In each blank, write the letter of the phrase that correctly identifies that person, group, place or thing.

1. ___ Woodrow Wilson
2. ___ Louis D. Brandeis
3. ___ Charles Evans Hughes
4. ___ Hiram Johnson
5. ___ Alfred Zimmerman
6. ___ Pope Benedict XV
7. ___ John J. Pershing
8. ___ St. Mihiel salient
9. ___ Meuse-Argonne Offensive
10. ___ Georges Clemenceau
11. ___ David Lloyd-George
12. ___ Czechoslovakia
13. ___ Henry Cabot Lodge

A) lost to Wilson in 1916 election; former governor of New York and Supreme Court Justice
B) Prime Minister of England who gave in to pressure to punish Germany
C) tried unsuccessfully to arrange conference for peace between world governments in 1917
D) Senate majority leader who was anti-Wilson and isolationist
E) created by Wilson in his attempt to give self-determination to Europe
F) "Black Jack"; General; commanded American Expeditionary Force in World War I
G) Supreme Court Justice; relativist in law and morality like Holmes
H) first distinctly U.S. offensive in World War I; begun September 12, 1918
I) promoted the League of Nations as an instrument to spread American principles of democracy and bring peace to the world
J) German Foreign Secretary who urged alliance with Mexico against the U.S.
K) Prime Minister of France; threatened to abandon League of Nations to get punishment of Germany
L) progressive Republican elected Governor of California in 1916
M) American offensive that stopped because of the Armistice

**Mini-Essay Question:** (Extra credit—4 points.) State what Wilson's policy of "self-determination" actually meant for European nations after World War I, and give three examples.

**Personal Opinion:** Name an important or interesting fact that you learned in this chapter. How could this fact affect your life?

**Supplemental Reading**

F. A. Forbes. *Pope St. Pius X.* TAN.

Warren H. Carroll. *The Rise and Fall of the Communist Revolution*. Christendom Press, Front Royal, Virginia.

# 21 *VIVA CRISTO REY!*

Text Pages 300-312

**Perfect Score: 100** **Score:** ________________
(Each Question is worth 2 points.)

## Completion

**Directions:** Complete and make each statement true and accurate by writing one or more words on each blank line.

1. The National Catholic Party and the League of Catholic ______________________ were attempts by young Catholics to persevere in their faith in the midst of Mexico's problems.

2. Wilson had an ______________________ (prohibition) placed on the selling of arms to Huerta, while openly giving aid to the revolutionaries, especially Villa.

3. U.S. meddling in Mexico in 1914 led to The ______________________ Incident, which almost erupted into war between Mexico and the United States.

4. Carranza could not enforce the provisions of the ______________________ of the Revolution which gave most of the governmental power to the president and which gave the government complete power over the Church.

5. As a result of the attempted bombing of the portrait of Our Lady of Guadalupe, Mexico City Catholics began daily ______________________ in reparation for the wrongs committed by the government.

6. The Obregon government expelled ______________________, the Pope's representative, for dedicating a monument to Christ the King, and later dispersed the Eucharistic Congress as part of its ongoing oppression of the Church.

7. In March of 1925, Mexican Catholics formed the National League for ______________________ Defense to defend the Church against the anti-Catholic government.

8. The brilliant young lawyer in Jalisco who pleaded with his followers to carry their crosses in defending the Church against the government, even if it would mean their blood, was Anacleto Gonzalez ______________________.

9. Because of their battle cry—*Viva Cristo Rey!*—the rebels were named the ______________________.

10. When Gonzalez Flores was executed on April 1, 1927, along with three other men who had been tortured with him, his last words echoed the last words of Garcia _______________________ : "I die, but God does not die. *Viva Cristo Rey!*"

11. Humberto and _______________________ Pro, who were brothers of Padre Miguel Pro and members of the NLDR, released balloons over Mexico City carrying anti-government leaflets.

12. Señora _______________________ and her servants saw Padre Pro elevated above the floor during a Mass not long before his arrest by the Calles government.

13. After Padre Pro gave his brothers absolution, he encouraged them to offer their lives together for the cause of religion in Mexico so that God would accept their _______________________ .

14. Father _______________________ of the U.S. National Catholic Welfare Conference met with President Calles at the request of Dwight Morrow in an effort to help end the Cristero revolt.

## Multiple Choice

**Directions:** After each statement below, there is a set of words or phrases. Circle the letter next to the one word or phrase that best completes the sentence.

1. At the end of the 19th century and at the beginning of the 20th century, Mexico enjoyed reasonable stability under the leadership of:
   a) Francisco Madera
   b) President Nuñez
   c) Porfirio Diaz
   d) Emiliano Zapata

2. The cruel leader of the bandit forces who robbed, tortured and killed poor and rich alike, and who was supported by Wilson in the early years of the Revolution in Mexico, was:
   a) Pancho Villa
   b) Victoriano Huerta
   c) Alvaro Obregon
   d) Emiliano Zapata
   e) Plutarco Calles

3. President Francisco Madera could not solve the problems in Mexico and was murdered by:
    a) Villa
    b) Huerta
    c) Obregon
    d) Zapata
    e) Calles

4. Almost all of the revolutionaries showed no respect for the Catholic Church, jailed bishops and religious and took over Church property. The one revolutionary leader in Mexico who had respect for the Church was:
    a) Villa
    b) Huerta
    c) Obregon
    d) Zapata
    e) Calles

5. The 1914 convention that Obregon set up resulted in failure, since none of the Revolutionary leaders there knew anything about government; shortly afterward, two of the leaders marched on Mexico City. They were:
    a) Villa and Carranza
    b) Obregon and Carranza
    c) Huerta and Zapata
    d) Villa and Zapata
    e) Villa and Obregon

6. The oppression of Catholics in Mexico in the 1920s included an exploding bomb at the Archbishop's residence in Mexico City and in Guadalajara, as well as a bomb which exploded but failed even to harm the glass in front of the portrait of Our Lady of Guadalupe. These occurrences happened during the government of:
    a) Huerta
    b) Obregon
    c) Calles
    d) Portes Gil
    e) Cardenas

7. The revolutionary president who made the statement, "I have a personal hatred for Christ," and proceeded to jail priests, close seminaries and convents, and severely oppress the Church was:
    a) Huerta
    b) Obregon
    c) Calles
    d) Portes Gil
    e) Cardenas

8. When approached by the NLDR leaders, American bishops refused to assist their uprising despite the intense persecution of Catholics throughout Mexico. Among these bishops were all of the following except the:
   a) Bishop of Boston, MA
   b) Bishop of Columbus, OH
   c) Bishop of Corpus Christi, TX
   d) Bishop of Baltimore, MD

9. The following priests gave their life in martyrdom in defense of the Faith in Mexico, with the exception of:
   a) Father José Genaro Sanchez
   b) Father Burke
   c) Father Matteo Correa Magallanes
   d) Father Miguel Pro
   e) Father David Uribe

10. The revolutionary leader who declared in 1924 that he stood for "the uprooting of religion" was:
   a) Villa
   b) Huerta
   c) Madera
   d) Carranza
   e) Calles

## True/False

**Directions:** Circle the letter T if the statement is true or F if the statement is false.

1. T F Alvaro Obregon was made into a kind of Mexican Robin Hood by the U.S. newspapers.
2. T F Cuba and Ecuador offered to arbitrate the dispute between Mexico and the U.S. in order to avert war, and Mexico and the U.S. accepted.
3. T F The outbreak of violence that resulted from Francisco Madera imprisoning Diaz is known in Mexico as The Revolution.
4. T F General John Pershing and the U.S. troops forced Villa into hiding in 1916, and he never again returned to the status he once had.
5. T F The bomb destined to destroy Juan Diego's tilma in the shrine of Our Lady of Guadalupe was almost the final blow to the Mexicans, who became very discouraged.
6. T F The Bishops of Mexico met with the NLDR leadership and agreed that armed resistance to the anti-Catholic government would be a just cause.

7. T F William F. Buckley refused to finance the NLDR uprising, because he did not agree with the cause of the Cristeros.

8. T F Padre Pro used disguises so he could bring the Sacraments to the people in Mexico City.

9. T F A young boy revealed under torture the hiding place of Padre Pro.

10. T F In 1929, the Mexican bishops came to an agreement with the Mexican government, and public worship was resumed.

11. T F President Portes Gil agreed to grant amnesty to the Cristeros for all past and present offenses, and the Mexican government kept this promise.

12. T F During the years 1931 to 1935, the government again persecuted Church activity, closing churches and restricting priests, so that the sacrifices of the Cristeros appeared to be in vain.

13. T F When Pope John Paul II visited Mexico in 1979, he disobeyed still-existing laws prohibiting the wearing of clerical garb on the streets and the public celebration of the liturgy by foreign priests.

## Matching

**Directions:** This list is made up of names of persons, groups, places and things. Each one corresponds to one of the lettered phrases below. In each blank, write the letter of the phrase that correctly identifies that person, group, place or thing.

1. ___ Francisco Madera
2. ___ Emiliano Zapata
3. ___ Venustiano Carranza
4. ___ Admiral Mayo
5. ___ Capistrán Garza
6. ___ Luis Batís
7. ___ William F. Buckley
8. ___ Pascual Diaz
9. ___ Anacleto Gonzalez Flores
10. ___ Dwight Morrow
11. ___ José de Leon Toral
12. ___ Emilio Portes Gil
13. ___ Manuel Avila Camacho

A) U.S. ambassador who believed Cristeros were mindless revolutionaries

B) insisted that Mexico publicly apologize to the U.S. in the Vera Cruz Incident

C) President of Mexico in 1940 who succeeded Cardenas; announced: "I am a believer."

D) NLDR leader; went to U.S. to solicit funds for the Catholic uprising against Calles

E) Inaugurated President of Mexico in 1917; proclaimed the Constitution of the Revolution

F) assassinated Obregon at a luncheon

G) lawyer; leader of Cristeros; tortured and executed on April 1, 1927

H) first Catholic priest martyred in Cristero rebellion in Mexico; cried "*Viva Cristo Rey!*" ("Long live Christ the King!")

I) Bishop of Tabasco exiled to U.S.; refused to endorse uprising of Catholics in Mexico

J) mestizo farmer; revolutionary leader who wanted justice/land for the Indians in Mexico

K) President of Mexico upon Porfirio Diaz's resignation; tried to solve problems with elections

L) Mexican President who had ex-Cristeros executed in 1930 after promising them amnesty

M) president of U.S. oil company; refused to finance NLDR uprising after speaking with exiled bishop

**Mini-Essay Question:** (Extra credit—4 points.) Summarize the incident involving miraculous protection of Our Lady of Guadalupe's portrait in 1921.

**Personal Opinion:** Name an important or interesting fact that you learned in this chapter. How could this fact affect your life?

**Supplemental Reading**

Fr. Wilfrid Parsons, S.J. *Mexican Martyrdom*. TAN.

Most Rev. Francis C. Kelley. *Blood Drenched Altars—A Catholic Commentary on the History of Mexico*. TAN.

Ann Ball. *Blessed Miguel Pro—20th Century Mexican Martyr*. TAN.

Bro. Charles Madden, O.F.M. *Freemasonry—Mankind's Hidden Enemy*. TAN.

Fr. Robert J. Fox. *Saints and Heroes Speak*, Vol. 4, pp. 131-142 (Blessed Miguel Pro). Fatima Family Apostolate.

# 22 BOOM, DEPRESSION AND THE NEW DEAL

Text Pages 313-335

**Perfect Score: 100** **Score:** ________________
(Each Question is worth 2 points.)

## Completion

**Directions:** Complete and make each statement true and accurate by writing one or more words on each blank line.

1. Because America had just been through war, its foreign policy during the 1920s reflected its wish to be left alone, that is, America was ______________________ in foreign policy.

2. When Warren Harding told Americans during his bid for the presidency in 1920 that America needed healing and ______________________, he captured the mood in America and coined this word to represent it.

3. The 1920s were a time when traditional standards of morality were ignored, and a false morality was imposed with the passing of the 18th Amendment, which prohibited the sale of ______________________.

4. In the 1920s, education was permeated by ______________________, the idea that discipline was bad because it took away the freedom of children. This idea spread from schools into homes.

5. In the 1920s, many Americans reacted violently against anything that differed from the dominant American culture, which was nicknamed the WASP culture: White Anglo-Saxon ______________________.

6. An organization known as the ______________________ used terrorism and political power against blacks, Catholics, Jews and immigrants; their tactics included burning crosses in front of homes and requiring all children to attend public schools.

7. The *Independent* Magazine lauded business as the solution to everything, and Calvin Coolidge stated: "The man who builds a factory builds a ______________________ . . . ." This type of false idealization and encouragement led to irresponsible stock market investment and buying on credit.

8. In the 1920's, the inflationary policies of the ______________________ System encouraged borrowers to borrow too much and bankers to loan too much.

9. The bad economic policies of the 1920s resulted in an artificial ______________________ or period characterized by business expansion, spending and investment.

10. Due to optimistic statements made by President ______________________ and his Secretary of the Treasury regarding the availability of easy money, bankers and investors, lulled into a false sense of security, continued in their imprudent level of loaning and investing.

11. President ______________________ was blamed for the economic miseries of the Depression, which had begun in 1929, during his term in office.

12. Under President ______________________, many government social programs were enacted in an effort to end the Depression, which would actually be ended only through World War II.

13. Through New Deal legislation, such as the Federal Emergency Relief Administration, the principle of ______________________, which had long been a part of American life and which was endorsed by the Popes, was abandoned in favor of provision by the federal government for problems that would have been better handled at the local level.

14. The ______________________ program, which provides payments for the elderly and disabled, also has the effect of discouraging thrift, eroding family responsibilities, and increasing Americans' dependence on the federal government.

## Multiple Choice

**Directions:** After each statement below, there is a set of words or phrases. Circle the letter next to the one word or phrase that best completes the sentence.

1. The document that renounced war as an instrument of national policy and was signed by 15 nations in August 1928 was named after the French Foreign Minister and the U.S. Secretary of State. It is known as the:
   a) Lodge-Denby Pact
   b) Kellogg-Briand Pact
   c) Dewey-Lenroot Pact
   d) none of the above

2. The 18th Amendment to the Constitution concerned Prohibition and took effect in 1920. The legislative act that implemented it was the:
   a) Prohibition Act
   b) Liquor Prohibition Act
   c) Volstead Act
   d) Illegal Drink Act
   e) none of the above

3. In the 1920s, the Ku Klux Klan had 5 million members and dominated the political systems in all of the following states except:
   a) Oklahoma
   b) Indiana
   c) Texas
   d) Oregon
   e) New York

4. The scandals of Warren Harding's administration were a result of his appointing friends to public office. The scandals involved all of the following except:
   a) protection of bootleggers
   b) the Teapot Dome oil reserves
   c) selling pardons and paroles
   d) selling offices
   e) the Houston regional oil reserves

5. Among the factors involved in the Great Inflation which preceeded the Depression were all of the following except:
   a) U.S. government statements about "easy money"
   b) excessive investing, using credit
   c) excessive saving by individuals
   d) excessive borrowing by businesses
   e) the approaching 1928 election

6. Roosevelt called a special session of Congress to meet five days after his inauguration in order to deal with the critical problem of bank closures. During this legislative session, Congress:
   a) passed the Emergency Banking Relief Act
   b) restricted government powers over banks so they would have more ability to work for the people
   c) adjourned shortly after the banks reopened, giving people confidence in Roosevelt's rapid-fire action
   d) a and b only
   e) a, b and c

7. The New Deal programs initiated by President Roosevelt aimed at fixing the nation's economic problems and restoring confidence in government. These programs included all of the following except:
   a) Federal Emergency Relief Administration (FERA)
   b) Agricultural Adjustment Administration (AAA)
   c) National Recovery Administration (NRA)
   d) Civilian Conservation Corps (CCC)
   e) Share Our Wealth Movement (SWM)

8. The government guaranteed individual bank deposits under $5,000 through the:
   a) Works Progress Administration (WPA)
   b) Federal Deposit Insurance Corporation (FDIC)
   c) Federal Emergency Relief Administration (FERA)
   d) Gold Repeal Joint Resolution
   e) none of the above

9. The clergyman from Detroit who hosted a weekly radio broadcast attacking both Communism and capitalism, who opposed the charging of high interest and who formed the National Union for Social Justice was:
   a) Rev. Gerald L. K. Smith
   b) Dr. Francis Townsend
   c) Floyd Olsen
   d) Fr. Charles Coughlin
   e) none of the above

10. President Roosevelt's New Deal policies had several effects, which included all of the following except:
    a) swift restoration of American confidence in the government
    b) ending of the Depression
    c) labor unions becoming a dominant force in America
    d) increased dependence on Washington
    e) erosion of family responsibilities

## True/False

**Directions:** Circle the letter T if the statement is true or F if the statement is false.

1. T F Eager for peace after World War I, the U.S. was one of the first nations to join the newly formed League of Nations to ensure freedom.

2. T F Americans in the 1920s had more leisure time to listen to the radio and attend movies and sports. Babe Ruth, Lou Gehrig and others were big hits, and Charles Lindbergh captured America's attention with his *Spirit of St. Louis*.

3. T F Harding collaborated in the selling of offices, pardons and paroles by the Ohio Gang; it was left to Coolidge to initiate reform.

4. T F The Depression which struck during Hoover's administration had been preceded by a period of inflation under Coolidge's administration.

5. T F After the stock market crash of 1929, Hoover's administration took deflationary measures that helped stabilize the economy.

6. T F The Dust Bowl occurred because of the failure of farmers to practice good conservation; however, the federal government was able to keep the farmers from serious financial loss.

7. T F Franklin Roosevelt broke precedent by giving the acceptance speech for his presidential nomination immediately at the Democratic convention, rather than later from his home, and by running for a third term as President.

8. T F Franklin Roosevelt's response to the Depression was immediate action by the federal government.

9. T F Hoover's "Fireside Chat" radio broadcasts helped restore confidence to the American people.

10. T F The Tennessee Valley Authority (TVA) was an excellent example of the federal government encouraging private individuals to solve their own economic problems.

11. T F When Roosevelt canceled the gold clause, the value of paper money declined and people were deprived of the full value of money that was rightfully theirs, so that the administration was in effect committing theft.

12. T F The goal of the Works Progress Administration (WPA) was to put people to work—on useful projects or on anything, whereas the Civilian Conservation Corps (CCC) was a useful program which did needed work in parks, forests and flood control projects.

13. T F In the struggle between Franklin Roosevelt and the Supreme Court over the constitutionality of various New Deal programs, the Court upheld a series of important New Deal measures, including the National Labor Relations Act and the Social Security laws.

# Matching

**Directions:** This list is made up of names of persons, groups, places and things. Each one corresponds to one of the lettered phrases below. In each blank, write the letter of the phrase that correctly identifies that person, group, place or thing.

1. ___ Al Capone
2. ___ Margaret Sanger
3. ___ John Dewey
4. ___ David C. Stephenson
5. ___ Al Smith
6. ___ James Farley
7. ___ Harry L. Hopkins
8. ___ Herbert Hoover
9. ___ Warren G. Harding
10. ___ Calvin Coolidge
11. ___ Franklin Delano Roosevelt
12. ___ Huey Long
13. ___ Charles Evans Hughes

A) "Grand Dragon" (leader) of the Ku Klux Klan
B) used the slogan, "A chicken in every pot and two cars in every garage."
C) pledged a "New Deal" for the American people
D) said America needed a return to "normalcy" after World War I
E) Catholic; Democratic candidate for president in 1928 and 1932
F) developed the theory of pragmatism in education, saying an idea is valuable if it works, regardless of truth
G) Chief Justice of the Supreme Court; Wilson's presidential opponent in 1916
H) criminal who controlled Cicero, Illinois in the 1920s
I) said, "I do not choose to run for President in 1928."
J) dictator-like Governor of Louisiana; led the Share Our Wealth Movement
K) Roosevelt's presidential campaign manager
L) New York social worker; administrator of FERA under Roosevelt
M) pushed for legalization of contraceptives to "help" the poor

**Mini-Essay Question:** (Extra credit—4 points.) Tell why no one wants to criticize the Social Security program, then state three problems that arise because of this program.

**Personal Opinion:** Name an important or interesting fact that you learned in this chapter. How could this fact affect your life?

**Supplemental Reading**

Charles Callan Tansill. *Back Door to War—The Roosevelt Foreign Policy, 1933-41.* Available from TAN.

# 23 THE UNITED STATES IN WORLD WAR II

Text Pages 337-361

**Perfect Score: 100** **Score:** ________________

(Each Question is worth 2 points.)

## Completion

**Directions:** Complete and make each statement true and accurate by writing one or more words on each blank line.

1. World War II began in 1939 when the Nazis attacked ______________________ and England and France came to its assistance.

2. Although not yet ready to enter the war, in September 1940 the U.S. transferred 50 destroyers to ______________________; in return, this nation gave the U.S. 99-year leases on bases in its territory.

3. On ______________________ (date), the day after the bombing of Pearl Harbor, the U.S. Congress declared war on Japan.

4. When the Japanese—who did not know how to deal with prisoners—marched 11,500 prisoners of war across the island of Corregidor in the Philippines, so many men died that the march became known as the ______________________ Death March.

5. The series of Japanese victories at the beginning of 1942 was finally halted at ______________________ Island, where U.S. victory and heavy Japanese losses marked the beginning of the end for Japan.

6. Under the Supreme Allied Commander, U.S. General ______________________, the U.S. and Great Britain had driven the Germans out of North Africa by May of 1943.

7. The policies agreed to by President Roosevelt and British Prime Minister Churchill in January of 1943 in Casablanca included the invasion of ______________________, the requirement of unconditional surrender, and terror bombing.

8. Terror or ______________________ bombing involved bombing cities rather than military targets, which meant the killing of innocent civilians, including women and children.

9. In an attempt to charm and appease the Communist dictator Josef Stalin at the conference in Teheran in November of 1943, Roosevelt endorsed the Communist takeover of Eastern ______________________, asking Stalin to keep the endorsement silent until after the 1944 presidential elections so that Roosevelt would not lose the votes of Polish Americans.

10. The brilliant rocket scientist ______________________ developed the V-1 and V-2 rockets for Hitler, but their development came too late to help Germany win the war.

11. Hitler ordered the execution of about 5,000 people after the ______________________ Conspiracy in Germany failed to assassinate him. U.S. newspapers refused to give any credit to those trying to resist Hitler.

12. After victory at Guadalcanal, the U.S. recaptured the Marianas, Guam and Saipan from the Japanese; the most important battle in this U.S. drive toward Japan was the Battle of the ______________________ Sea against Admiral Ozawa.

13. Like Wilson before him, Roosevelt at Yalta was willing to give up freedom for whole countries of people (including Poland, Bulgaria and Romania) in order to obtain endorsement for his proposed international organization, the ______________________, even though Wilson's League of Nations had already failed.

14. The forcible return of over two million Russians to Communist Russia, where the Russians would face execution or slave labor camps, was carried out by American and British soldiers at gunpoint as one of the provisions of the Yalta agreements and is known as ______________________.

## Multiple Choice

**Directions:** After each statement below, there is a set of words or phrases. Circle the letter next to the one word or phrase that best completes the sentence.

1. On March 11, 1941, the U.S. passed legislation which Roosevelt had proposed earlier that year, allowing certain countries to receive arms and supplies from the U.S. This legislation was the:
   a) America First Committee
   b) Atlantic Charter
   c) Manhattan Project
   d) Lend-Lease Act
   e) none of the above

2. The "four freedoms"—"freedom from want and fear, freedom of speech and religion"—as well as opposition to the imposition of any government against the will of its people, were included in Roosevelt and Churchill's:
   a) Atlantic Charter
   b) Freedom Declaration
   c) Manhattan Project
   d) Yalta Conference
   e) Casablanca Conference

3. The U.S. ships which sunk during the Japanese attack on Pearl Harbor included:
   a) the Arizona
   b) the California
   c) the Houston
   d) a and b only
   e) a and c only

4. The United States began its offensive attack against Japan with a landing by the U.S. Marines on August 7, 1942 at:
   a) Midway Island
   b) Bataan Peninsula
   c) Guadalcanal
   d) Leyte Gulf
   e) Samar

5. Although the Italian government surrendered September 8, 1943, the battle for Italy between the Allies and the Germans was not over. The U.S. Fifth Army landed at Salerno and fought with even cooks and supply personnel on the line in what was known as:
   a) Operation Avalanche
   b) Operation Italy
   c) Bloody Ridge
   d) The Dora Line
   e) Battle of the Bulge

6. Operation Overlord is considered the most important operation of the war; this operation involved the Allied invasion on "D-Day" of:
   a) Rome, Italy
   b) Monte Cassino, Italy
   c) Guadalcanal, Solomon Islands
   d) Normandy, France
   e) Berlin, Germany

7. The two beaches assigned to U.S. troops in the invasion of D-Day were code-named:
   a) Utah and Arizona
   b) Utah and Omaha
   c) Arizona and California
   d) Arizona and Utah
   e) none of the above

8. Eisenhower's failure to guard the Ardennes resulted in the Germans attacking and advancing against Allied lines on December 16, 1944 at the following battle:
   a) Battle of the Bulge
   b) Battle of Leyte Gulf
   c) Battle of Midway Island
   d) First Cassino
   e) Second Cassino

9. When General MacArthur returned to the Philippines in October of 1944, he led the fight for the islands in the following naval battle—which set a record for the number of ships fighting in a naval battle:
   a) The Battle of Bataan
   b) The Battle of Leyte Gulf
   c) The Battle of Midway Island
   d) The Battle of Corregidor
   e) none of the above

10. When American and British forces were ordered to allow Russian troops to reach Berlin first, Communists gained control over:
   a) Poland and Bulgaria
   b) Hungary and Yugoslavia
   c) Poland and Hungary
   d) Poland and Czechoslovakia
   e) eastern Germany and Czechoslovakia

## True/False

**Directions:** Circle the letter T if the statement is true or F if the statement is false.

1. T F The Atlantic Charter was endorsed by 15 nations, including the Soviet Union—which never intended to keep the Charter's provisions.

2. T F The struggle for Guadalcanal showed the superiority of Japanese air power and the superiority of U.S. naval power.

3. T F The Allies destroyed the monastery of Monte Cassino during the attack known as Second Cassino because the Germans had been using the monastery as a headquarters.

4. T F In World War II, the U.S., Great Britain and the Soviet Union (Allies or Allied Forces) fought against Germany, Italy and Japan (Axis Powers).

5. T F A Japanese *Banzai* charge consisted of a series of suicide dives by kamikaze pilots.

6. T F Although World War II began originally because the British (and French) were trying to protect Poland's independence, British Prime Minister Churchill cooperated with Roosevelt in allowing the Communists to absorb eastern Poland.

7. T F Soviet control of naval bases in Asia, and the use of Germans in forced labor after the war were among the concessions made by Roosevelt and Churchill to Stalin at the Yalta conference.

8. T F Firebombing of civilian targets ceased because of the outrage in Parliament after the killing of about 135,000 innocent people including refugees in Dresden, Germany, a city which had no military significance.

9. T F Hitler committed suicide about a week before Field Marshall Jodl signed the document of unconditional surrender, and May 8, 1945 was officially designated V-E Day, the formal end of the War against Germany.

10. T F The agreement of the Yalta Conference requiring citizens of an Allied country who were liberated by another Allied country to be sent back to their homeland benefitted Vlasov's Army and the Cossacks.

11. T F Truman had no choice but to consider using the atomic bomb, since the Japanese were unwilling to negotiate surrender.

12. T F After 100,000 people were killed by the first atomic bomb, which was dropped over Hiroshima, a second was dropped on Nagasaki, Japan, which was the most Catholic city in Japan.

13. T F Although U.S. troops fought courageously in World War II, the United States under Roosevelt and Truman committed evils of firebombing non-combatants, using atomic bombs on cities, sending people back to lands of Communism to face almost certain death, and agreeing to allow Communists to establish tyrannical rule over eastern European countries which were Catholic.

# Matching

**Directions:** This list is made up of names of persons, groups, places and things. Each one corresponds to one of the lettered phrases below. In each blank, write the letter of the phrase that correctly identifies that person, group, place or thing.

1. ___ Charles Lindbergh
2. ___ Douglas MacArthur
3. ___ General Wainwright
4. ___ Victor Emmanuel
5. ___ General Erwin Rommel
6. ___ Major David Martin
7. ___ Louis P. Lochner
8. ___ Werner von Braun
9. ___ General Montgomery
10. ___ Alger Hiss
11. ___ Albert Einstein
12. ___ Admiral William Leahy
13. ___ Captain Robert Lewis

A) brilliant scientist who developed V-1 and V-2 rockets for Germany
B) flew B-29 bomber *Enola Gay*, which dropped bomb on Hiroshima
C) brilliant German tank commander; nicknamed "The Desert Fox"
D) German Jewish scientist who informed Roosevelt about the atomic bomb
E) member of anti-Hitler movement in Germany whom Roosevelt refused to speak to
F) vehemently opposed use of the Atom bomb as modern barbarism
G) planned the failed Operation Market Garden, which ended with severe casualties
H) King of Italy who formed a new government under Marshal Badoglio after the fall of Mussolini
I) Commander-in-Chief of U.S. forces in the Far East
J) presidential adviser who Roosevelt relied on at Yalta Conference; a Communist
K) commanded troops which held out for two months against Japanese at Bataan
L) aviation hero who led the America First Committee; isolationist
M) "Man Who Never Was"; body with a fictitious identity to trick Hitler

**Mini-Essay Question:** (Extra credit—4 points.) Explain how the secret agreement at the Yalta Conference between Roosevelt, Churchill and Stalin concerning citizens of an Allied country who had been liberated by another Allied country affected Vlasov's army and the Cossacks. Include a description of what Operation Keelhaul was and how it got its name.

**Personal Opinion:** Name an important or interesting fact that you learned in this chapter. How could this fact affect your life?

**Supplemental Reading**

Samuel Eliot Morison. *History of United States Naval Operations in World War II.*

# 24 THE BIRTH AND DEATH OF ANTI-COMMUNISM

Text Pages 363-388

**Perfect Score: 100** **Score:** ______________

(Each Question is worth 2 points.)

## Completion

**Directions:** Complete and make each statement true and accurate by writing one or more words on each blank line.

1. After the tremendous success of the Marshall Plan, giving comprehensive aid to the initial 16 European countries, the U.S. and Great Britain decided to extend the program to Germany as well. As a result, the Soviets imposed a full-scale blockade on the city of ______________________ . The U.S. and Germany began a massive airlift, and finally the Soviets lifted the blockade.
2. In May 1949, the German ______________________ Republic (West Germany) was formed, with its capital city being established at Bonn. The Soviets retaliated by setting up the German Democratic Republic (East Germany) as a Soviet satellite state.
3. Thanks to the U.S. policy of supplying economic and military aid to nations threatened by Communist takeovers (a policy later called "containment"), as delineated in the ______________________ Doctrine, Greece and Turkey were able to maintain their independence.
4. The conflict between the U.S. and the U.S.S.R. which began after World War II based on the U.S.'s acknowledgement of an obligation to preserve freedom (from Communism) throughout the world is known as the ______________________ .
5. When General George ______________________ went to China in 1945 announcing Truman's plan for a coalition government between Nationalists and Communists, the Nationalist Chiang Kai-shek (a Christian and anti-Communist) refused to participate. Therefore, the U.S. stopped giving aid to Chiang Kai-shek, while the Communist leader Mao Tse-tung received much aid from the Soviet Union.
6. Mao Tse-tung conquered Peking in 1949 and set up the "People's Republic of China" while Chiang Kai-shek fled to the island of ______________________ (then called Formosa) to set up a free Chinese government there: the U.S. had failed to prevent Mao's setting up a brutal dictatorship in mainland China, where he slaughtered millions and outlawed the practice of religion.

7. Alger Hiss changed his strategy twice: first denying that he knew Chambers, then claiming he had known him superfically by the name of George Crosley, then outright attacking Chambers, insinuating in one of his questions that Chambers was ______________________ —an insinuation which, unfortunately, the public believed (especially since they wanted to deny the truth about Hiss).

8. Julius and Ethel ______________________ were executed by electric chair in 1953 for conspiracy to commit espionage, i.e., passing atomic secrets to the Soviet Union. This incident became a powerful propaganda tool in the hands of the Communists, who made the two look like martyrs (a common Communist tactic).

9. When Communist North Korea invaded free South Korea in 1950, the U.N. was able to approve U.S. intervention because the ______________________ delegate to the U.N. Security Council, who would have vetoed the resolution, was boycotting the Council. Liberal leaders had ruined U.S. military preparedness through legislation and policy directives.

10. Because of American control of the air and sea during the Korea War, the U.S. was able to hold the ______________________ Perimeter against the Communists.

11. The U.S. forces in Korea had to face not only North Korean soldiers but also Communist ______________________ soldiers, who inflicted heavy casualties on U.S. Marines, as well as suffering heavy casualties themselves.

12. The dividing line between North Korea and South Korea at the beginning of the Korean War in 1950 was the ______________________ parallel; at the truce talks (1951-1953), it soon became obvious that both sides were willing to let the boundary remain where it had been when the war began.

13. After the United States stood firm against Communism in the Korean War, the Communists turned from fighting conventional wars, changing their tactics for world domination to guerrilla warfare and terrorism, disguised as ______________________ .

14. With Eisenhower's refusal to aid the ______________________ Freedom Fighters in 1956, Eastern Europe was left unaided and thus fell to Communist domination. Because liberal shapers of public opinion presented a favorable view of Communism, eventually the American public came to believe that Communism was not so bad, a view that was reflected in American foreign policy.

# Multiple Choice

**Directions:** After each statement below, there is a set of words or phrases. Circle the letter next to the one word or phrase that best completes the sentence.

1. The German satellites confiscated by the Soviets at the Potsdam Conference in 1945 included all of the following except:
   a) Poland
   b) Romania
   c) Bulgaria
   d) Hungary

2. The Marshall Plan assisted European countries with massive aid after World War II and was named after George Marshall, who was:
   a) Vice President
   b) Secretary of State
   c) a Senator
   d) Secretary of Defense
   e) none of the above

3. The following very prominent and respected member of the Washington establishment, an architect of the U.N. and one of President Roosevelt's closest advisors at Yalta, was named by Whittaker Chambers as a Communist:
   a) Harry Gold
   b) Julius Rosenberg
   c) David Greenglass
   d) Alger Hiss
   e) Klaus Fuchs

4. All of the following men contributed to the U.S. turning against Chiang Kai-shek in favor of Mao Tse-tung, except for:
   a) Harry Dexter White
   b) Owen Lattimore
   c) John Stewart Service
   d) Alger Hiss
   e) Roy Cohn

5. Thanks to the Third Battalion, 5th Marine Division, the U.S. mission at this location was successful; as a result, General MacArthur and South Korean President Syngman Rhee re-established the government in Seoul, Korea:
   a) port of Inchon
   b) port of Pusan
   c) Kunu-ri Pass
   d) Chosin Reservoir
   e) Pork Chop Hill

6. Although the Chinese had been told to kill the Marines as they would kill snakes in their homes, the Marines were not so easy to get rid of. The men of the following Marine Division fought ferociously, held their positions, fought their way out of a trap, rescued their fellow Marines, brought out every one of their wounded men and marched into Hagaru having inflicted 37,400 casualties on the Communists and having effectively eliminated four Red Chinese armies from the war:
   a) First Marine Division
   b) Second Marine Division
   c) Third Marine Division
   d) Eighth Marine Division

7. When General MacArthur publicly attacked Truman after the President had refused to allow him to bomb the enemy supply lines on mainland (Communist) China, Truman fired MacArthur and appointed as the new commander-in-chief:
   a) William F. Dean
   b) Walt Phillips
   c) Matthew Ridgeway
   d) none of the above

8. American prisoners of war in Korea were treated so badly that at this particular prison camp, within eight months half of them had died—including all of the chaplains, who were singled out for particularly terrible treatment:
   a) Pork Chop Hill
   b) Heartbreak Ridge
   c) Death Valley
   d) Bloody Ridge
   e) none of the above

9. An Irish-German Catholic, Joseph McCarthy fought Communism because he knew that it was a real enemy to the Faith and to all decent values. Most of the persons whom he named as security risks were in fact security risks. All of the following are true about McCarthy except:
   a) he reacted emotionally and sometimes lost his temper
   b) he was mentally unbalanced and tended toward cruelty
   c) he named names and spoke out forcefully against those he believed to be Communists.
   d) he was attacked by the liberal leadership elite of America
   e) he was accused of creating a "climate of fear"

10. One of the security risks whom McCarthy identified had played a large role in formulating U.S. policy toward China; the Senate Subcommittee on Internal Security called this man "a conscious, articulate instrument of the Communist conspiracy." He was:
   a) Alger Hiss
   b) William Fulbright
   c) Joseph Alsop
   d) Irving Peress
   e) Owen Lattimore

# True/False

Directions: Circle the letter T if the statement is true or F if the statement is false.

1. T F The United States' firmness in supplying Germany with relief forced the Soviets to back down and lift their blockade on Berlin in May of 1949.

2. T F Konrad Adenauer was the strong Catholic Chancellor of the newly formed West German government who believed in the family and the natural law. Under his strong leadership, West Germany recovered economically and culturally.

3. T F NATO (the North Atlantic Treaty Organization) was formed to protect Western Europe from Communist aggression. General Eisenhower was established as commander of the NATO military force.

4. T F Throughout the Cold War, the United States went on the offensive against the Communists in an effort to spread Western values and liberate countries.

5. T F *Pacific Affairs*, a publication of the Institute for Pacific Relations (IPR), was sympathetic to Chiang Kai-shek and greatly influenced public opinion in the United States.

6. T F In 1948, the U.S. Congress voted to send a shipment of armaments to Chiang Kai-shek, but the Defense Department sent guns that were missing parts and planes without fuel.

7. T F North Korea's army was known as the North Korean People's Army (NKPA); South Korea was known as the Republic of Korea (ROK).

8. T F The U.S. was in an excellent state of military preparedness for the Korean War, due to the military build-up during World War II.

9. T F General MacArthur led the U.S. and the ROK in trying to drive the Communists completely out of the Korean peninsula, but he did not count on the Chinese Communists coming to help the North Koreans.

10. T F Eighty percent of the Chinese prisoners of war preferred to stay in the custody of Americans after the Korean War rather than be returned to their homeland.

11. T F The term "McCarthyism" came to mean meddling in the affairs of other people.

12. T F President Eisenhower was firm in protecting the rights of POW's to refuse to return to their home countries.

13. T F Austria's liberation in 1955 was the only instance since World War II when Soviet troops ever retreated (until Afghanistan in 1989).

# Matching

**Directions:** This list is made up of names of persons, groups, places and things. Each one corresponds to one of the lettered phrases below. In each blank, write the letter of the phrase that correctly identifies that person, group, place or thing.

1. ___ Mao Tse-tung
2. ___ Chiang Kai-shek
3. ___ Harry Dexter White
4. ___ Whittaker Chambers
5. ___ Lloyd Paul Stryker
6. ___ Thomas Murphy
7. ___ Allen Weinstein
8. ___ Harry Gold
9. ___ General William F. Dean
10. ___ Millard Tydings
11. ___ Walter Lippmann
12. ___ Joseph Welch
13. ___ John Foster Dulles

A) lawyer of Alger Hiss who called Chambers a moral leper

B) Eisenhower's Secretary of State; assisted in saving Austria from communism

C) American chemist in espionage ring with Klaus Fuchs, the Rosenbergs, etc.; code-named Raymond

D) Senator; headed committee that investigated McCarthy's charges; biased against McCarthy

E) Christian leader of the Nationalists in China; set up free Chinese government in Taiwan

F) Army lawyer; repeatedly attacked McCarthy and Roy Cohn to discredit them

G) U.S. commanding officer of 24th Infantry Division in Korean War; received Congressional Medal of Honor

H) Communist leader of People's Republic of China

I) Catholic government prosecutor who assisted in getting Alger Hiss convicted

J) political columnist; assisted in discrediting McCarthy with the public

K) former Communist; gave Christian witness before the House Un-American Activities Committee

L) Assistant Secretary of the Treasury; thwarted economic aid to Chiang

M) author of *Perjury: The Hiss-Chambers Case*; corroborated Chambers' testimony

**Mini-Essay Question:** (Extra credit—4 points.) Explain how Whittaker Chambers and Joseph McCarthy suffered because of their confrontation of the evil of Communism, and give one good result of their sacrifices.

**Personal Opinion:** Name an important or interesting fact that you learned in this chapter. How could this fact affect your life?

**Supplemental Reading**

Anthony Kubek. *How the Far East Was Lost: American Policy and the Creation of Communist China, 1941-1949.*

Richard Reeves. *The Life and Times of Joe McCarthy.*

# 25 COMMUNISTS VS. CHRISTIANS IN LATIN AMERICA

Text Pages 390-399

**Perfect Score: 100** **Score:** ________________

(Each Question is worth 2 points.)

## Completion

**Directions:** Complete and make each statement true and accurate by writing one or more words on each blank line.

1. Instead of teaching the students the truth, the University of ______________________ in Cuba promoted liberal and Marxist ideas.

2. Upon his release from prison for his first attempt to overthrow the government (July 1953), Castro collected funds in the United States for his revolution and recruited followers for the 26th of ______________________ Movement.

3. As soon as Castro became Communist dictator of Cuba, the upper and middle classes fled to the United States mostly to the state of ______________________ .

4. Under President Eisenhower's administration, Cuban exiles were trained in ______________________ America to invade Cuba and overthrow Castro.

5. When the USSR sent bombers and missiles to Cuba in 1962, it was a tactical move to get the United States to make concessions over ______________________ ; however, when the U.S. Navy blockaded Cuba, Kennedy reached a compromise with Khruschev and the Soviets to withdraw their missiles.

6. Cuba became a base for missile-bearing ______________________ for the Soviet Union.

7. The regime of Juan Perón, which tried to put into effect Catholic social doctrine by encouraging private industry, private property and social justice for the poor, was known as the ______________________ .

8. When Juan Perón forbade Evita from running for vice-president, she told the people of Argentina that she would not exchange one battle position for another, and August 22, 1951, became known as her "Day of ________________________."

9. The Basilica of the Virgen de ________________________ is a national shrine in Argentina, where the country was dedicated to the Immaculate Heart of Mary. Although destined for Buenos Aires, the people felt the Virgin Mary wanted the statue to remain in the little town where the car it was transported in broke down since no one was able to lift the statue, as it became very heavy.

10. When pro- ________________________ were elected in Chile, Americans' beliefs regarding the election of officials through the democratic process caused them to feel that the new leaders were rightful rulers, even though evil ones.

11. Chile's Minister of the ________________________ led an attack on the hidden vehicles when the truckers on strike went to attend a meeting scheduled with Allende's government in August 1973.

12. Because of Allende's cruelty, Edmundo Searle was tortured, blinded, and was deprived of water, food and ________________________, leaving him physically and mentally scarred for life.

13. After Allende's defeat, Pinochet and the new Chilean government led a national ________________________ to the Shrine of the Blessed Mother in which two and a half million Chileans participated, in their relief and gratitude at being delivered from Communism.

14. Through the intercession of Our Lady of Guadalupe, all the Latin American countries except for ________________________ were successful in the fight against Communism in the 20th century.

# Multiple Choice

**Directions:** After each statement below, there is a set of words or phrases. Circle the letter next to the one word or phrase that best completes the sentence.

1. To escape Castro's invasion, Batista and his followers fled to this country in January of 1959:
   a) Argentina
   b) Chile
   c) Ecuador
   d) Dominican Republic

2. Castro nationalized almost everything in Cuba including:
   a) utilities
   b) banks
   c) large industries
   d) medium industries
   e) all of the above

3. The Cuban exiles invaded Cuba on April 17, 1961 at the site of:
   a) the Cordillera of the Andes
   b) the Sierra Maestra
   c) the Bay of Pigs
   d) Casa Rosada
   e) La Moneda

4. The Eva Perón foundation not only dispensed money to the poor, it also undertook all of the following except:
   a) setting up hospitals and a nursing school
   b) campaigns against tuberculosis and malaria
   c) setting up clinics and nursing homes
   d) health checkups and a soccer league for children
   e) campaigns against smallpox

5. After Evita's death in July 1952, Juan Perón changed and turned against the Church, taking measures that opposed the Church, including all of the following except:
   a) restricting activities of priests
   b) legalizing divorce
   c) proposing to end the Church's participation in public education
   d) threatening to tax Church property

6. The presidential residence of Argentina, which Juan Carlos Onganía seized in 1966 from the liberal government before dedicating the country to the Immaculate Heart of Mary, was known as the:
   a) Peronata
   b) Casa Rosada
   c) Plaza de Mayo
   d) La Moneda
   e) none of the above

7. The wife of Juan Perón who succeeded him in July 1974 upon his death did not have the ability to keep the country in order, and she was overthrown by the military in 1976. She was:
   a) Evita
   b) Rosita
   c) Francesca
   d) none of the above

8. The name of the Chilean political party under Allende, which cheated in the 1973 elections by forging voter ID cards, stealing more than 100,000 votes, was:
   a) *Patria y Libertad*
   b) *Unidad Popular*
   c) *Patria Popular*
   d) none of the above

9. The Chilean generals fortunately discovered and stopped the plot by Allende to kill 50,000 traditionalists. This plot was called:
   a) Plan A
   b) Plan B
   c) Plan T
   d) Plan Z
   e) none of the above

10. After Allende committed suicide in 1973, the new government of Chile, comprised of five generals, four of whom were Catholic, achieved all of the following except:
   a) purging the government criminals
   b) rebuilding the economy
   c) gaining the support of the Chilean bishops
   d) opening seminaries
   e) arresting the Communists

# True/False

**Directions:** Circle the letter T if the statement is true or F if the statement is false.

1. T F Because the U.S. dominated Cuba and its government after the Spanish-American War, Cuba adopted materialism and secularism, making the Church's influence there weak.

2. T F In 1958, the U.S. continued to support Batista and his efforts to maintain the government because it recognized that Castro, a Communist, would be dangerous.

3. T F When Castro took over Cuba in January 1959, his extemporaneous speeches and his personality captivated the Cubans and eliminated all opposition to his rule.

4. T F Castro, following the example of Communist leaders before him, sought to destroy families primarily through taking the mother out of the home to work and the children out of the home to be placed in boarding schools which indoctrinated them with Communism.

5. T F Through Che Guevara, Castro was largely successful in taking the revolution outside of Cuba and converting other Latin American countries.

6. T F Because Kennedy listened to liberals and withdrew the order to the U.S. planes to give air cover to the Cuban exiles invading the island (1961), many Cubans died or were taken prisoner by the Communists.

7. T F Because Juan and Eva Perón assisted the lower classes in Argentina, the poor were not tempted to Marxism as a solution to problems, as has been the case in many other countries.

8. T F Evita Perón, who worked 18-hour days administering aid to the poor, died in 1952 of cancer. She was mourned by the Argentineans, who petitioned the Pope to canonize her, and her autobiography was made required reading in the public schools.

9. T F Juan Carlos Onganía was a good Catholic but unfortunately a poor leader of government, and in 1970 he was overthrown.

10. T F The Peronist Party dissolved when Juan Perón's third wife was overthrown by a military coup in 1976.

11. T F After Evita's death, Juan Perón turned against the Church. Peronistas attacked Buenos Aires churches, setting fires and smashing statues. These sacrileges got Juan Perón excommunicated. He was forced to resign as President of Argentina.

12. T F Hospitals and medicine were the one aspect of life that improved under Salvador Allende and his Communist regime. Infant mortality was cut in half.

13. T F Allende arranged to sell Chile's entire gold reserve on the black market and keep the income, bankrupting the country.

## Matching

**Directions:** This list is made up of names of persons, groups, places and things. Each one corresponds to one of the lettered phrases below. In each blank, write the letter of the phrase that correctly identifies that person, group, place or thing.

1. ___ Fulgencio Batista
2. ___ Fidel Castro
3. ___ Che Guevara
4. ___ Nikita Khruschev
5. ___ Ramón Castillo
6. ___ Juan Perón
7. ___ Evita
8. ___ CGT
9. ___ Eduardo Frei
10. ___ Salvador Allende
11. ___ Edmundo Searle
12. ___ *La Moneda*
13. ___ Augusto Pinochet

A) Argentinian labor organization which supported Evita for vice-president
B) corrupt dictator of Argentina whom the military overthrew in June 1943
C) wife of Juan Perón; had authority over all charities in Argentina
D) lied to get elected in Chile in 1970; leader of *Unidad Popular* party
E) leader of the military junta in Chile with four other generals after Allende's death
F) Communist terrorist who tried to lead revolts in Latin American countries; accomplice of Castro
G) took over the Cuban government in 1952; fled from Castro in 1959
H) President of Chile in the 1960s; leader of Christian Democratic Party
I) presidential palace in Chile
J) President of Argentina from 1946 to 1955
K) Soviet dictator who reached a compromise with Kennedy in 1962 Cuban Missile Crisis
L) leader of *Patria y Libertad* who was tortured by the Allende regime
M) former law student at the University of Havana who established a Communist government in Cuba in 1959

**Mini-Essay Question:** (Extra credit—4 points.) How did the actions of the U.S. undermine Cuban resistance to Communism?

**Personal Opinion:** Name an important or interesting fact that you learned in this chapter. How could this fact affect your life?

**Supplemental Reading**

Joseph A. Page. *Peron: A Biography.*

# 26 THE MORAL DECLINE OF AMERICA

Text Pages 400-426

**Perfect Score: 100** **Score:** ______________
(Each Question is worth 2 points.)

## Completion

**Directions:** Complete and make each statement true and accurate by writing one or more words on each blank line.

1. By its frequent declaration of laws as unconstitutional, the Supreme Court led by Chief Justice ____________________ was able to effectively legislate. Before this Court, it was rare for the Supreme Court to declare laws unconstitutional.
2. In the 1963 Schempp-Murray cases regarding school prayer, "strict ____________________ " toward religion was the policy that the Supreme Court said government should pursue in public life.
3. In proclaiming a "New Frontier" in his inaugural speech, John F. Kennedy stated, "Ask not what your country can do for you. Ask what you can do for your ____________________."
4. The French fought the Communists in Vietnam until 1954, when they negotiated the independence of Laos and Cambodia and divided Vietnam into two parts, with Ho Chi Minh in place as the leader of a Communist government in North Vietnam and Ngo Dinh ____________________ in South Vietnam.
5. Many Buddhists burned themselves to death in 1963, as part of a special suicide promotion group under the leadership of the pro-Communist ____________________, so that Americans would believe that Diem's regime must be tyrannical if people were willing to die in protest against it.
6. Martin Luther King, Jr., who began the Civil Rights Movement, believed in nonviolent, passive ____________________ and moral pressure to end discrimination against blacks.

7. When Johnson tried to save South Vietnam from the Communists in 1965, Congress passed the ______________________ Gulf Resolution. Initially a few battalions of Marines were sent, and on June 27, 1965, the first American combat troops were sent.

8. There were many reasons for the agitation in 1968 in the United States that brought the country close to ______________________ . The Vietnam War, the civil rights movement, Great Society promises regarding poverty, the mass media and moral relativism agitated students, Blacks, war protesters and those in society in general.

9. In January 1968, with the ______________________ offensive by the Communists in South Vietnam, and continuing through the siege of Khe Sanh, the liberal media falsely portrayed the U.S. as losing the Vietnam War, and finally Johnson succumbed to pressure to get out of the war.

10. While there were riots on the campuses of the University of California before this, the largest campus riot began in 1968 in New York at ______________________ University, where the students occupied the administration building, taking three hostages.

11. The policy of ______________________ adopted by Nixon so that he could remain popular with the public aimed to achieve "friendly" relations with the Soviet Union and Red China.

12. The push for legal abortion was the result of the sexual revolution and accompanying moral decline of the late 1960s and of the feminist or Women's ______________________ Movement.

13. The case of Roe v. Wade challenged the constitutionality of the criminal abortion statute in the state of ______________________, where the single pregnant woman known as "Roe" lived. At that time, this state and most other states prohibited abortion unless it was deemed necessary to save the life of the mother.

14. The "Reagan Doctrine" provided assistance to anti-Communist freedom fighters in ______________________, Angola and Nicaragua and sought to weaken the Soviet Union.

# Multiple Choice

**Directions:** After each statement below, there is a set of words or phrases. Circle the letter next to the one word or phrase that best completes the sentence.

1. The first major case was brought before the Warren Court in May 1954 and had to do with segregation in schools. This case is known as:
   a) Schempp-Murray
   b) Brown v. Topeka Board of Education
   c) Roe v. Wade
   d) none of the above

2. This first major case of the Warren Court was the beginning of the Supreme Court's practice of (in effect) writing laws and of making social changes that is known as:
   a) Supreme Court legalism
   b) Supreme Court activism
   c) judicial activism
   d) judicial legalism
   e) none of the above

3. Kennedy's foreign policy problems included all the following except:
   a) situation in Cuba
   b) Iranian hostage crisis
   c) Communists building a wall dividing Berlin
   d) situation in Vietnam

4. These Great Society programs under Johnson were created in order to help the poor and elderly pay medical bills:
   a) Medicaid
   b) War on Poverty program
   c) Medicare
   d) a and c only
   e) a, b and c

5. Federal education, job training, and employment programs put forth under Johnson were part of:
   a) a War on Poverty
   b) Medicaid
   c) Aid-to-education
   d) Medicare
   e) the Civil Rights Movement

6. All are reasons the United States had problems in Vietnam except:
   a) the bombing was unsuccessful
   b) the blockade of Haiphong Harbor caused havoc for U.S. troops
   c) U.S. trade with Soviet Russia increased while Russian Communists were arming North Vietnam
   d) U.S. soldiers could not pin down the enemy

7. Those who were guilty of involvement in the Watergate scandal during the Nixon administration included all of the following except:
   a) John Dean
   b) Gerald Ford
   c) Attorney General Mitchell
   d) Robert Haldeman
   e) John Ehrlichman

8. The push for abortion began in the states, with the first state legislature to legalize it (in 1966) being that of the state of:
   a) California
   b) North Carolina
   c) Colorado
   d) Texas
   e) New Mexico

9. The 7-2 vote by the Supreme Court on January 22, 1973, declaring all laws prohibiting abortion to be unconstitutional, asserted a woman's constitutional "right" to abortion over a child's right to life. Their decision included three points: the due process clause of the Fourteenth Amendment, a "right of privacy," and the denial of the personhood or rights of unborn children. All of the justices except for the following endorsed the decision written by Justice Blackmun:
   a) Lewis Powell and Warren Burger
   b) Thurgood Marshall and Byron White
   c) Potter Stewart and William Brennan
   d) William O. Douglas and William Brennan
   e) William Rehnquist and Byron White

10. President Bill Clinton authorized the following on January 22, 1993, shortly after taking office:
    a) fetal experimentation
    b) abortions in military hospitals
    c) investigations leading to the approval of RU-486
    d) the use of tax dollars to fund abortion and contraceptives overseas
    e) all of the above

# True/False

**Directions:** Circle the letter T if the statement is true or F if the statement is false.

1. T F Instead of trying to find support for their decisions in previous cases or in the words of the Constitution, the Warren Court used the justice's own opinions as a basis for making decisions and declaring laws unconstitutional.

2. T F During his 1960 presidential election campaign, Kennedy made it clear that his Catholic faith would have an important part in his governmental life and in his decisions as president.

3. T F The Nixon-Kennedy debates on television established the visual media as key in presidential campaigns.

4. T F The National Liberation Front was a group of South Vietnamese who wanted to be free of Diem's rule and who joined in the VietCong's kidnapping, killing of village leaders, guerrilla warfare and raids.

5. T F The Vietnamese had built their society on discipline and respect for authority, not elections. Not understanding this, liberal Americans stirred up agitation against Diem because he had not been democratically elected.

6. T F The U.S. ambassador to Vietnam, Henry Cabot Lodge, supported the decision of the anti-Diem agitators in the U.S. who said that if Diem did not release Buddhist rebels, the U.S. would encourage the overthrow of Diem. Diem was killed, and martial law was invoked more often in the two years following his death than in the nine years of his rule.

7. T F The documents of the Second Vatican Council were orthodox, but some passages could be seen as ambiguous, and liberals spread their own ideas as "The Spirit of Vatican II."

8. T F The encyclical *Humanae Vitae*, reaffirming that contraception is intrinsically immoral and that the Church cannot and will never change this teaching, was issued by Pope John Paul II.

9. T F Nixon was the third President in U.S. history to resign.

10. T F U.S. Ambassador in Saigon, Grew, turned down Admiral Gayler's offer and stopped General Smith's attempt to help evacuate the South Vietnamese, thereby sentencing many Vietnamese to murder or torture in prison camps when the Communists occupied Saigon, renaming it Ho Chi Minh City.

11. T F Jimmy Carter's administration censured the People's Republic of China while encouraging the Nationalist Chinese government in Taiwan and handled the Iranian hostage crisis quickly and effectively.

12. T F The acceptance of contraception and abortion is leading to acceptance of assisted suicide and euthanasia. Spiritual renewal must take place in order for these problems to be corrected.

13. T F During Pope John Paul II's visit to the United States in 1979, he defended the value of each person when addressing the United Nations; he told bishops to teach absolute values and reject compromises with the modern world, and he asked parents to give their children brothers and sisters rather than material goods.

## Matching

**Directions:** This list is made up of names of persons, groups, places and things. Each one corresponds to one of the lettered phrases below. In each blank, write the letter of the phrase that correctly identifies that person, group, place or thing.

1. ___ Earl Warren
2. ___ Richard Daley
3. ___ Lee Harvey Oswald
4. ___ Jack Ruby
5. ___ Mark Rudd
6. ___ Ralph Abernathy
7. ___ Robert Kennedy
8. ___ Hubert Humphrey
9. ___ George Wallace
10. ___ Ayatollah Kohmeni
11. ___ Ronald Reagan
12. ___ Gerald Ford
13. ___ William Casey

A) appointed Vice President after Spiro Agnew's forced resignation; became President upon Nixon's resignation in 1974

B) dictatorial leader of Iran who refused to communicate with Carter during Iranian hostage crisis

C) Senator killed by Jordanian Arab Sirhan Sirhan in 1968

D) president of Columbia University's Students for a Democratic Society (revolutionary campus group) in 1968

E) Alabama Governor; candidate for the American Party in 1968 presidential race; shot by Arthur Bremer

F) pro-Communist who assassinated Kennedy in Dallas, TX on November 22, 1963

G) signed a bill when Governor that permitted abortion on demand; later apologized and became pro-life advocate

H) Martin Luther King's successor as head of Southern Christian Leadership Conference; led "March of the Poor" in 1968

I) CIA director who assisted Ronald Reagan in weakening the Soviet Union

J) Lyndon Johnson's Vice President; liberal Democrat who lost election to Nixon in 1968

K) California Governor whom Eisenhower appointed Chief Justice of the Supreme Court in 1953

L) Dallas night club owner who murdered Oswald

M) Chicago Mayor; engineered massive vote fraud so that Kennedy could win over Nixon in 1960

**Mini-Essay Question:** (Extra credit—4 points.) Give five of the results of the spreading of liberal ideas in "The Spirit of Vatican II," with many Catholics and Catholic leaders succumbing to secularism and other temptations instead of meeting these challenges with strengthened faith.

**Personal Opinion:** Name an important or interesting fact that you learned in this chapter. How could this fact affect your life?

# ANSWER KEY

## Chapter 1: THE NEW WORLD MEETS THE OLD (Pages 1-5)

**Completion**

1. Neolithic or Agricultural
2. collectivized
3. serpent
4. devil
5. Chile
6. San Salvador
7. four
8. Ferdinand; Isabel
9. Catholic
10. Brazil
11. Demarcation
12. Florida
13. Cuba
14. Amerigo Vespucci

**Multiple Choice**

| | | | |
|---|---|---|---|
| 1. | b | 6. | c |
| 2. | a | 7. | c |
| 3. | d | 8. | a |
| 4. | d | 9. | b |
| 5. | b | 10. | d |

**True/False**

| | | | |
|---|---|---|---|
| 1. | F | 8. | F |
| 2. | F | 9. | F |
| 3. | T | 10. | T |
| 4. | T | 11. | F |
| 5. | F | 12. | F |
| 6. | T | 13. | F |
| 7. | F | | |

**Matching**

| | | | |
|---|---|---|---|
| 1. | H | 8. | M |
| 2. | D | 9. | A |
| 3. | J | 10. | I |
| 4. | G | 11. | E |
| 5. | B | 12. | K |
| 6. | L | 13. | C |
| 7. | F | | |

**Mini-Essay Question**

*Any two:*

1. False gods were worshipped instead of the one True God.
2. Aztecs lived in a culture of death. Since society revolved around satisfying the appetites of the devil gods they worshiped with the sacrifice of living human beings, especially innocent children (estimates of 1 out of every 5 children).
3. The individual person was taught that he or she was nothing. People could not own land, but instead worked so the wealthy could live in luxury. Boys were enslaved or killed if they did not become warriors. There was no freedom, only fear and slavery.

---

## Chapter 2: TWO HEROES: CORTES AND MAGELLAN (Pages 7-12)

**Completion**

1. 15 million
2. faith
3. hosts
4. human skulls
5. greed
6. Sorrow
7. Indian
8. Charles I
9. South America
10. Victory
11. Lucia
12. Straits
13. Philippines
14. Spice

**Multiple Choice**

| | | | |
|---|---|---|---|
| 1. | b | 6. | e |
| 2. | a | 7. | d |
| 3. | b | 8. | c |
| 4. | e | 9. | b |
| 5. | a | 10. | a |

**True/False**

| | | | |
|---|---|---|---|
| 1. | T | 8. | F |
| 2. | F | 9. | T |
| 3. | F | 10. | T |
| 4. | F | 11. | F |
| 5. | F | 12. | T |
| 6. | T | 13. | T |
| 7. | T | | |

**Matching**

| | | | |
|---|---|---|---|
| 1. | E | 8. | C |
| 2. | J | 9. | H |
| 3. | L | 10. | F |
| 4. | D | 11. | K |
| 5. | M | 12. | G |
| 6. | B | 13. | A |
| 7. | I | | |

**Mini-Essay Question**

Both were devout Catholics who lived their faith in daily life and who had a spiritual purpose to their endeavors. Both were courageous, daring and determined. Both were great, competent leaders who faced incredible odds and hardships, terrible setbacks, and still accomplished their mission. Both contributed greatly to the Old World's discovery of the New World.

## Chapter 3: MISSIONARIES AND CONQUISTADORS (Pages 13-18)

**Completion**

1. governing
2. Twelve
3. music
4. Honduras
5. Isabel
6. roses
7. twenty
8. villages
9. Texas
10. Mississippi
11. Lima
12. Argentine
13. Cortés
14. New Spain

**Multiple Choice**

| | | | |
|---|---|---|---|
| 1. | b | 6. | d |
| 2. | c | 7. | b |
| 3. | b | 8. | c |
| 4. | a | 9. | a |
| 5. | d | 10. | d |

**True/False**

| | | | |
|---|---|---|---|
| 1. | F | 8. | T |
| 2. | F | 9. | T |
| 3. | T | 10. | F |
| 4. | T | 11. | F |
| 5. | F | 12. | T |
| 6. | T | 13. | F |
| 7. | F | | |

**Matching**

| | | | |
|---|---|---|---|
| 1. | A | 8. | I |
| 2. | L | 9. | M |
| 3. | G | 10. | J |
| 4. | F | 11. | C |
| 5. | E | 12. | B |
| 6. | K | 13. | H |
| 7. | D | | |

**Mini-Essay Question**

Cortés conquered an oppressive dictatorship at odds of 10,000 to one; eliminated human sacrifice and cannibalism; established a just government; established a land policy; fostered unity between two peoples; encouraged culture; explored Central America and Lower California; encouraged missionary activity.

---

## Chapter 4: BRINGING CHRIST TO THE NEW WORLD (Pages 19-25)

**Completion**

1. Jesuits
2. Apostle
3. Superior
4. penance
5. Archbishop
6. Santa Fe
7. 50
8. Lopez
9. reductions
10. Dutch
11. England
12. cabildos
13. Black Legend
14. Mexico

**Multiple Choice**

| | | | |
|---|---|---|---|
| 1. | d | 6. | a |
| 2. | d | 7. | b |
| 3. | a | 8. | e |
| 4. | d | 9. | c |
| 5. | b | 10. | d |

**True/False**

| | | | |
|---|---|---|---|
| 1. | F | 8. | F |
| 2. | T | 9. | F |
| 3. | T | 10. | T |
| 4. | F | 11. | T |
| 5. | T | 12. | T |
| 6. | F | 13. | T |
| 7. | F | | |

**Matching**

| | | | |
|---|---|---|---|
| 1. | D | 8. | E |
| 2. | M | 9. | H |
| 3. | J | 10. | L |
| 4. | C | 11. | B |
| 5. | G | 12. | F |
| 6. | K | 13. | I |
| 7. | A | | |

**Mini-Essay Question**

1. Christianity was the greatest benefit that the Spanish brought to the New World. The Spanish stopped idolatry, human sacrifice and cannibalism and brought Christ and His Catholic Church to the Indians. Latin America remains Catholic.
2. Failure to train a native clergy is the greatest weakness noted. As a result, the Church in the New World was governed only by people of European descent.

---

## Chapter 5: FRANCE IN THE NEW WORLD (Pages 27-33)

**Completion**

1. Hapsburg
2. Jean
3. Relations
4. Associates
5. Charles I
6. feast
7. sufferings
8. dispensation
9. Mohawks
10. consecration
11. King's
12. sinner
13. catfish
14. Biloxi

**Multiple Choice**

| | | | |
|---|---|---|---|
| 1. | c | 6. | b |
| 2. | e | 7. | c |
| 3. | a | 8. | e |
| 4. | d | 9. | c |
| 5. | d | 10. | a |

**True/False**

| | | | |
|---|---|---|---|
| 1. | F | 8. | F |
| 2. | F | 9. | T |
| 3. | T | 10. | F |
| 4. | T | 11. | F |
| 5. | T | 12. | T |
| 6. | F | 13. | F |
| 7. | T | | |

**Matching**

| | | | |
|---|---|---|---|
| 1. | H | 8. | L |
| 2. | C | 9. | G |
| 3. | I | 10. | A |
| 4. | B | 11. | E |
| 5. | M | 12. | J |
| 6. | F | 13. | D |
| 7. | K | | |

**Mini-Essay Question**

1. Father Isaac Jogues
2. René Goupil
3. Jean de Lalande
4. Father Jean Brébeuf
5. Father Gabriel Lalemant
6. Father Anthony Daniel
7. Father Charles Garnier
8. Father Noel Chabanel

## Chapter 6: FROM ENGLAND TO AMERICA (Pages 35-40)

**Completion**

1. Spain
2. Roanoke
3. London
4. tobacco
5. legislature
6. Compact
7. written
8. Catholic
9. Messianism
10. Delaware
11. Charter
12. Toleration
13. France
14. Bourbon

**Multiple Choice**

| | | | |
|---|---|---|---|
| 1. | a | 6. | a |
| 2. | d | 7. | b |
| 3. | c | 8. | b |
| 4. | d | 9. | c |
| 5. | a | 10. | d |

**True/False**

| | | | |
|---|---|---|---|
| 1. | T | 8. | T |
| 2. | T | 9. | T |
| 3. | F | 10. | F |
| 4. | F | 11. | F |
| 5. | F | 12. | T |
| 6. | F | 13. | T |
| 7. | T | | |

**Matching**

| | | | |
|---|---|---|---|
| 1. | C | 8. | L |
| 2. | G | 9. | I |
| 3. | A | 10. | M |
| 4. | J | 11. | H |
| 5. | D | 12. | B |
| 6. | E | 13. | K |
| 7. | F | | |

**Mini-Essay Question**

Prior to this time, the English had not really been interested in the New World except for fishing expeditions. Henry's disobedience (not accepting the authority of the Church regarding the indissolubility of marriage) led to his forming the Church of England (the Anglican church). This resulted in religious differences and the persecution of many sects under his daughter Elizabeth. Due to religious intolerance in England, these people colonized North America to a large extent and were intolerant of the Catholics who came to settle there. When King William and Queen Mary made Maryland a royal colony, Catholics were excluded from civil rights, and in 1692, the Act of Religion sealed the doom of the Maryland experiment. Catholicism was outlawed in Maryland.
(Author's note: Had Henry VIII not led England into schism and begun a new church, it is likely that the Americas would have been settled almost entirely by Catholics.)

---

## Chapter 7: THE EVE OF AMERICAN WAR FOR INDEPENDENCE (Pages 41-46)

**Completion**

1. representative
2. charter
3. Townshend
4. Intolerable
5. Suffolk
6. divinity
7. liberal
8. Catholic
9. Maryland
10. Jefferson
11. providence
12. religion
13. Protestant
14. people

**Multiple Choice**

| | | | |
|---|---|---|---|
| 1. | a | 6. | c |
| 2. | b | 7. | b |
| 3. | d | 8. | c |
| 4. | b | 9. | e |
| 5. | d | 10. | e |

**True/False**

| | | | |
|---|---|---|---|
| 1. | F | 8. | T |
| 2. | F | 9. | T |
| 3. | T | 10. | T |
| 4. | F | 11. | F |
| 5. | F | 12. | F |
| 6. | T | 13. | T |
| 7. | F | | |

**Matching**

| | | | |
|---|---|---|---|
| 1. | G | 8. | K |
| 2. | D | 9. | B |
| 3. | F | 10. | E |
| 4. | H | 11. | A |
| 5. | J | 12. | I |
| 6. | L | 13. | C |
| 7. | M | | |

**Mini-Essay Question**

*Any three:*

1. Liberalism rejects moral absolutes, emphasizing that men should be free to do whatever they want in moral matters.
2. Liberalism rejects authority, especially religious authority.
3. Liberalism is usually opposed to hereditary monarchy.
4. According to Liberalism, political authority comes from the people themselves.
5. According to Liberalism, the people should be free to overthrow existing governments, by violence if necessary, and to set up new governments based on the will of the majority, as interpreted and guided by intellectual leaders.

The central fact regarding all authority which liberalism ignores:
All authority comes from God, and if authority is not exercised in harmony with God's law, it is not legitimate.

## Chapter 8: THE UNITED STATES' WAR FOR INDEPENDENCE (Pages 47-52)

**Completion**

1. Continental
2. Congress
3. four
4. Lee
5. Lee
6. Christmas
7. disperse
8. Louis XVI
9. redoubts
10. Cornwallis
11. Carleton
12. Washington
13. values
14. Vernon

**Multiple Choice**

| | | | |
|---|---|---|---|
| 1. | e | 6. | b |
| 2. | a | 7. | e |
| 3. | a | 8. | c |
| 4. | b | 9. | b |
| 5. | d | 10. | e |

**True/False**

| | | | |
|---|---|---|---|
| 1. | F | 8. | F |
| 2. | T | 9. | T |
| 3. | T | 10. | T |
| 4. | T | 11. | T |
| 5. | F | 12. | F |
| 6. | F | 13. | F |
| 7. | F | | |

**Matching**

| | | | |
|---|---|---|---|
| 1. | L | 8. | D |
| 2. | I | 9. | G |
| 3. | F | 10. | E |
| 4. | A | 11. | M |
| 5. | K | 12. | H |
| 6. | B | 13. | C |
| 7. | J | | |

**Mini-Essay Question**

A revolution is a total upheaval of government, values and way of life, destroying moral standards and civilized order. Since the Americans were not changing these things but were instead fighting to keep their traditional way of government, and since their independence made little or no difference in their values or way of life, this war was not properly a "revolution." Rather, since the Americans were fighting for independence from a British government which had become increasingly tyrannical, defending their traditions against British aggression, the war is accurately called the "American War for Independence."

---

## Chapter 9: THE BIRTH OF THE AMERICAN GOVERNMENT (Pages 53-58)

**Completion**

1. Congress
2. federal
3. borrowed
4. Critical
5. Federalists
6. Constitutional
7. Connecticut
8. convention
9. Federalist
10. Christian
11. sovereignty
12. Church
13. morality
14. Electoral

**Multiple Choice**

| | | | |
|---|---|---|---|
| 1. | b | 6. | d |
| 2. | d | 7. | b |
| 3. | d | 8. | b |
| 4. | c | 9. | c |
| 5. | a | 10. | d |

**True/False**

| | | | |
|---|---|---|---|
| 1. | F | 8. | F |
| 2. | F | 9. | T |
| 3. | T | 10. | F |
| 4. | F | 11. | F |
| 5. | T | 12. | T |
| 6. | T | 13. | T |
| 7. | F | | |

**Matching**

| | | | |
|---|---|---|---|
| 1. | I | 8. | A |
| 2. | E | 9. | H |
| 3. | M | 10. | C |
| 4. | K | 11. | F |
| 5. | B | 12. | D |
| 6. | J | 13. | G |
| 7. | L | | |

**Mini-Essay Question**

No. In the 20th century, the national (federal) government began to take power from the states. Also, various branches of the government began dominating other branches. An example of this is the fact that the Judiciary branch (which interprets the Constitution) gained dominance in the mid-20th century, so that the Supreme Court became virtually absolute, with no real check on its power.

## Chapter 10: CATHOLICS IN THE NEW NATION (Pages 59-64)

**Completion**

1. office
2. First
3. Mary
4. Georgetown
5. Smith
6. Louisiana
7. Administrator
8. trusteeism
9. indifferentism
10. Protestant
11. Cheverus
12. tuberculosis
13. St. Catherine Labouré
14. U.S. Catholic Miscellany

**Multiple Choice**

| | | | |
|---|---|---|---|
| 1. | e | 6. | b |
| 2. | e | 7. | c |
| 3. | e | 8. | e |
| 4. | d | 9. | c |
| 5. | a | 10. | b |

**True/False**

| | | | |
|---|---|---|---|
| 1. | F | 8. | T |
| 2. | F | 9. | T |
| 3. | F | 10. | T |
| 4. | F | 11. | F |
| 5. | T | 12. | T |
| 6. | T | 13. | F |
| 7. | T | | |

**Matching**

| | | | |
|---|---|---|---|
| 1. | L | 8. | C |
| 2. | D | 9. | K |
| 3. | H | 10. | B |
| 4. | J | 11. | F |
| 5. | A | 12. | I |
| 6. | M | 13. | G |
| 7. | E | | |

**Mini-Essay Question**

*Any two*:

1. religious indifferentism (the belief that one religion is as good as another or that a person is free to choose to practice no religion at all)
2. the belief that the Church should not interfere in politics (*Or*: a situation where moral values are precluded from the public conversation)
3. rejection of spiritual loyalty to the Holy Father

---

## Chapter 11: THE FRENCH REVOLUTION AND THE NEW WORLD (Pages 65-70)

**Completion**

1. Cuba
2. slaves
3. empire
4. Haiti
5. French Revolution
6. Thomas Jefferson
7. XYZ
8. Sedition
9. party
10. Thomas Jefferson
11. John Adams
12. Judiciary
13. privateers
14. Ghent

**Multiple Choice**

| | | | |
|---|---|---|---|
| 1. | d | 6. | c |
| 2. | b | 7. | a |
| 3. | b | 8. | d |
| 4. | c | 9. | a |
| 5. | c | 10. | d |

**True/False**

| | | | |
|---|---|---|---|
| 1. | F | 8. | T |
| 2. | F | 9. | F |
| 3. | T | 10. | F |
| 4. | F | 11. | T |
| 5. | F | 12. | F |
| 6. | T | 13. | F |
| 7. | F | | |

**Matching**

| | | | |
|---|---|---|---|
| 1. | D | 8. | A |
| 2. | F | 9. | E |
| 3. | K | 10. | I |
| 4. | B | 11. | L |
| 5. | J | 12. | G |
| 6. | M | 13. | C |
| 7. | H | | |

**Mini-Essay Question**

In the view known as "judicial supremacy," the Supreme Court becomes the paramount branch of government, with supremacy over the other two branches (executive and legislative) and over the States. The Supreme Court gains this supremacy through its power to declare laws and actions by the other two branches and by the States to be unconstitutional (contrary to the U.S. Constitution) and therefore forbidden; thus the Supreme Court's decisions become, in effect, "laws."

## Chapter 12: SPAIN IS DRIVEN FROM LATIN AMERICA (Pages 71-76)

**Completion**

1. Bourbons
2. Argentina
3. Church
4. democracy
5. Tumusla
6. liberal
7. Echavarri
8. Seminole
9. Transcontinental
10. Monroe
11. Hands-Off
12. Ipiranga
13. power
14. bureaucracies

**Multiple Choice**

| | | | |
|---|---|---|---|
| 1. | d | 6. | b |
| 2. | d | 7. | d |
| 3. | d | 8. | c |
| 4. | a | 9. | a |
| 5. | b | 10. | e |

**True/False**

| | | | |
|---|---|---|---|
| 1. | F | 8. | F |
| 2. | T | 9. | F |
| 3. | F | 10. | F |
| 4. | F | 11. | F |
| 5. | T | 12. | T |
| 6. | F | 13. | F |
| 7. | T | | |

**Matching**

| | | | |
|---|---|---|---|
| 1. | L | 8. | B |
| 2. | C | 9. | M |
| 3. | J | 10. | I |
| 4. | F | 11. | H |
| 5. | A | 12. | D |
| 6. | G | 13. | K |
| 7. | E | | |

**Mini-Essay Question**

*Any three:*

1. The Indians lost their land.
2. Control of the missions was taken from the Franciscans and the missions fell into disuse.
3. The economy fell into chaos.
4. Violence became more common than under Spanish rule, as factions were no longer held in check by religion and tradition.
5. Violence and instability increased also because of the armies left over from the wars of independence.
6. Creole aristocrats now held power and usually exercised it less wisely and with less restraint than had the Spaniards.
7. Government bureaucracies would grow rapidly (because the faction in power would give offices to friends and relatives).
8. Government became extremely costly, leading to inflation.
9. Government became unstable since factions out of power were tempted to try to gain power.

---

## Chapter 13: MANIFEST DESTINY (Pages 77-82)

**Completion**

1. Whigs
2. bargain
3. secede
4. Texas
5. Alamo
6. cheap
7. Manifest Destiny
8. Veracruz
9. Oregon
10. polygamy
11. Young
12. Veracruz
13. Guadalupe Hidalgo
14. slavery

**Multiple Choice**

| | | | |
|---|---|---|---|
| 1. | a | 6. | e |
| 2. | d | 7. | a |
| 3. | b | 8. | e |
| 4. | c | 9. | d |
| 5. | c | 10. | c |

**True/False**

| | | | |
|---|---|---|---|
| 1 | F | 8. | T |
| 2. | T | 9. | F |
| 3. | F | 10. | T |
| 4. | T | 11. | F |
| 5. | F | 12. | T |
| 6. | F | 13. | F |
| 7. | T | | |

**Matching**

| | | | |
|---|---|---|---|
| 1. | C | 8. | L |
| 2. | J | 9. | F |
| 3. | M | 10. | A |
| 4. | I | 11. | K |
| 5. | D | 12. | G |
| 6. | H | 13. | B |
| 7. | E | | |

**Mini-Essay Question**

*Any three*:

1. the desire of the slave states to legalize slavery in the empty lands and to regain some of the power they were losing in Congress because of the more rapid population growth in the North
2. the desire of land speculators to get rich selling the uninhabited lands
3. the desire of industrialists for new markets
4. the desire for adventure and excitement
5. the desire by quite ordinary people for cheap land and the chance to make a new start in life
6. the desire for security by eliminating foreign powers from U.S. borders
7. Manifest Destiny: the idea that the U.S. must spread its system of government across the Continent because that was its God-given destiny

## Chapter 14: NO IRISH NEED APPLY (Pages 83-88)

**Completion**

1. Nativism
2. Pope
3. Ursuline
4. ignorance
5. education
6. doctrine
7. convert
8. nativist
9. Protestants
10. German
11. Redemptorist
12. education
13. disharmony
14. Philadelphia

**Multiple Choice**

| | | | |
|---|---|---|---|
| 1. | c | 6. | e |
| 2. | a | 7. | d |
| 3. | e | 8. | b |
| 4. | d | 9. | a |
| 5. | d | 10. | c |

**True/False**

| | | | |
|---|---|---|---|
| 1. | T | 8. | T |
| 2. | F | 9. | F |
| 3. | F | 10. | F |
| 4. | F | 11. | F |
| 5. | T | 12. | T |
| 6. | T | 13. | T |
| 7. | F | | |

**Matching**

| | | | |
|---|---|---|---|
| 1. | G | 8. | A |
| 2. | D | 9. | K |
| 3. | I | 10. | B |
| 4. | L | 11. | E |
| 5. | C | 12. | H |
| 6. | M | 13. | F |
| 7. | J | | |

**Mini-Essay Question**

Pope Leo XIII condemned the following propositions of the Americanist Heresy:

1. the Holy Spirit guides people so they do not need the Sacraments or organized Church structure
2. the natural virtues are higher than the supernatural virtues
3. the active life is better than the contemplative life
4. religious vows are a restriction on freedom
5. the Church needs to accommodate its doctrines and practices to attract more Americans to it

---

## Chapter 15: THE COMING OF THE CIVIL WAR (Pages 89-94)

**Completion**

1. three-fifths
2. Maine
3. Quakers
4. Moderate
5. Texas
6. Constitution
7. District of Columbia
8. Whigs
9. arsenal
10. Sumter
11. Union
12. McDowell
13. Anaconda
14. perpetual

**Multiple Choice**

| | | | |
|---|---|---|---|
| 1. | a | 6. | e |
| 2. | c | 7. | d |
| 3. | b | 8. | c |
| 4. | d | 9. | e |
| 5. | a | 10. | e |

**True/False**

| | | | |
|---|---|---|---|
| 1. | T | 8. | F |
| 2. | T | 9. | T |
| 3. | F | 10. | F |
| 4. | F | 11. | F |
| 5. | T | 12. | T |
| 6. | T | 13. | F |
| 7. | F | | |

**Matching**

| | | | |
|---|---|---|---|
| 1. | D | 8. | E |
| 2. | K | 9. | H |
| 3. | C | 10. | L |
| 4. | G | 11. | F |
| 5. | M | 12. | B |
| 6. | I | 13. | J |
| 7. | A | | |

**Mini-Essay Question**

Other goals of the South:

1. independence
2. preservation of its land and culture from Northern capitalism and greed

Other goals of the North *(any two)*:

1. to preserve (or reunite) the Union
2. to demonstrate the superiority of American government
3. to whip the South

## Chapter 16: THE CIVIL WAR (Pages 95-100)

### Completion

1. Confederacy
2. Richmond
3. Rappahanock
4. Longstreet
5. Round
6. ammunition
7. Grant
8. Chickamauga
9. Wilderness
10. Appomattox
11. McLean
12. six
13. democratic
14. *habeas corpus*

### Multiple Choice

| | | | |
|---|---|---|---|
| 1. | d | 6. | b |
| 2. | a | 7. | b |
| 3. | e | 8. | d |
| 4. | d | 9. | d |
| 5. | d | 10. | d |

### True/False

| | | | |
|---|---|---|---|
| 1. | T | 8. | T |
| 2. | F | 9. | F |
| 3. | T | 10. | F |
| 4. | T | 11. | T |
| 5. | T | 12. | F |
| 6. | F | 13. | T |
| 7. | F | | |

### Matching

| | | | |
|---|---|---|---|
| 1. | C | 8. | D |
| 2. | I | 9. | G |
| 3. | F | 10. | B |
| 4. | A | 11. | E |
| 5. | L | 12. | H |
| 6. | J | 13. | K |
| 7. | M | | |

### Mini-Essay Question

The Emancipation Proclamation was an announcement issued in 1862 by President Lincoln declaring the freedom of all the slaves in rebel areas, though exempting the slaves in border states. The Emancipation Proclamation did not have an immediate effect. Southerners ignored it. It hurt Lincoln politically, and the Democrats were victorious in the November elections. The Emancipation Proclamation was criticized both by people who considered it too harsh and by those who considered it too lenient—leading to dissatisfaction with President Lincoln.

---

## Chapter 17: TRADITIONALISTS IN LATIN AMERICA (Pages 101-106)

### Completion

1. civil
2. United States
3. Reform
4. moratorium
5. Carlota (or Charlotte)
6. revolutionary
7. revenues
8. capitalists
9. hacendados
10. Confession
11. Christianize
12. Peru
13. concordat
14. balanced

### Multiple Choice

| | | | |
|---|---|---|---|
| 1. | b | 6. | d |
| 2. | b | 7. | d |
| 3. | c | 8. | a |
| 4. | c | 9. | e |
| 5. | a | 10. | b |

### True/False

| | | | |
|---|---|---|---|
| 1. | F | 8. | T |
| 2. | F | 9. | F |
| 3. | F | 10. | T |
| 4. | T | 11. | F |
| 5. | T | 12. | F |
| 6. | F | 13. | T |
| 7. | T | | |

### Matching

| | | | |
|---|---|---|---|
| 1. | L | 8. | B |
| 2. | D | 9. | E |
| 3. | G | 10. | I |
| 4. | M | 11. | K |
| 5. | C | 12. | J |
| 6. | H | 13. | A |
| 7. | F | | |

### Mini-Essay Question

The U. S. government supported Benito Juarez's rebel faction that constantly agitated and disturbed the order that Maximilian and Carlota were trying to achieve. The U.S. supplied arms and ammunition to Juarez, who finally captured and executed Maximilian in June 1867. The French government's failure to maintain its promise and keep its troops stationed in Mexico for a full three years led to complete vulnerability for Mexico and attack by rebel forces. France's constant emphasis on repayment of debt was a source of tremendous stress to Maximilian and Carlota. When Napoleon III would not listen to Carlota during the two times she came to plead with him, she knew that her mission and their government in Mexico had failed, and she became inconsolably paranoid. The stress was overwhelming and she collapsed into insanity.

## Chapter 18: THE UNITED STATES IN THE GILDED AGE (Pages 107-112)

**Completion**

1. Reconstruction
2. Southern
3. Indians
4. ratify
5. impeached
6. Democratic
7. money
8. patronage
9. Populist
10. Working
11. Charity
12. New Mexico
13. 238
14. Father De Smet

**Multiple Choice**

| | | | |
|---|---|---|---|
| 1. | b | 6. | b |
| 2. | e | 7. | a |
| 3. | a | 8. | c |
| 4. | a | 9. | e |
| 5. | c | 10. | e |

**True/False**

| | | | |
|---|---|---|---|
| 1. | T | 8. | T |
| 2. | F | 9. | F |
| 3. | T | 10. | T |
| 4. | T | 11. | T |
| 5. | F | 12. | F |
| 6. | T | 13. | T |
| 7. | F | | |

**Matching**

| | | | |
|---|---|---|---|
| 1. | G | 8. | F |
| 2. | D | 9. | J |
| 3. | K | 10. | H |
| 4. | M | 11. | B |
| 5. | C | 12. | E |
| 6. | I | 13. | L |
| 7. | A | | |

**Mini-Essay Question**

Father Pierre-Jean De Smet advocated gradual development of agricultural programs that would allow the Indians time to adjust to the new way of life. The U.S. government did not listen, but instead violated its treaties, took away Indian lands, shot Indians and burned their homes. Consequently, the Indians rebelled. Father De Smet begged the government to keep its promises to the Indians, refusing to negotiate with them unless the government did so. Instead, the government violated treaty after treaty, and as the Indians saw all of their lands taken away, they fought to keep the little they could. They were outnumbered and outgunned. Many were killed and some were banished to Oklahoma.

---

## Chapter 19: THE AGE OF THEODORE ROOSEVELT (Pages 113-118)

**Completion**

1. Klondike
2. DeLome
3. Maine
4. *Jungle*
5. Government
6. compulsory
7. convenient
8. Panama
9. Corollary
10. Mother Cabrini (Frances Cabrini)
11. Molokai
12. New Orleans
13. Blessed Sacrament
14. Maryknoll

**Multiple Choice**

| | | | |
|---|---|---|---|
| 1. | b | 6. | e |
| 2. | c | 7. | e |
| 3. | d | 8. | b |
| 4. | a | 9. | a |
| 5. | d | 10. | e |

**True/False**

| | | | |
|---|---|---|---|
| 1. | T | 8. | T |
| 2. | F | 9. | F |
| 3. | T | 10. | F |
| 4. | F | 11. | F |
| 5. | F | 12. | T |
| 6. | F | 13. | T |
| 7. | T | | |

**Matching**

| | | | |
|---|---|---|---|
| 1. | D | 8. | E |
| 2. | G | 9. | M |
| 3. | C | 10. | B |
| 4. | L | 11. | H |
| 5. | F | 12. | K |
| 6. | J | 13. | I |
| 7. | A | | |

**Mini-Essay Question**

Oliver Wendell Holmes, Jr. influenced the Supreme Court away from using moral principles as a basis for making decisions, toward using the individual feelings of the justices to make decisions. He served for 30 years and taught many young lawyers his philosophy. His influence can be seen throughout history, as the Supreme Court has made decisions in the way that he set forth, without regard to the laws of God (the Natural Law or the Divine Positive Law).

## Chapter 20: WOODROW WILSON AND THE FIRST WORLD WAR (Pages 119-124)

**Completion**

1. Princeton
2. unalterable
3. Freedom
4. bonds
5. regional
6. conservative
7. foreign
8. democracy
9. Kerensky
10. Fourteen
11. Austria
12. Versailles
13. Christianity/Christ
14. Communists

**Multiple Choice**

| | | | |
|---|---|---|---|
| 1. | c | 6. | e |
| 2. | c | 7. | b |
| 3. | e | 8. | b |
| 4. | a | 9. | c |
| 5. | a | 10. | b |

**True/False**

| | | | |
|---|---|---|---|
| 1. | T | 8. | F |
| 2. | F | 9. | T |
| 3. | F | 10. | F |
| 4. | T | 11. | F |
| 5. | T | 12. | F |
| 6. | F | 13. | T |
| 7. | T | | |

**Matching**

| | | | |
|---|---|---|---|
| 1. | I | 8. | H |
| 2. | G | 9. | M |
| 3. | A | 10. | K |
| 4. | L | 11. | B |
| 5. | J | 12. | E |
| 6. | C | 13. | D |
| 7. | F | | |

**Mini-Essay Question**

Wilson's policy of "self-determination" for European nations after World War I really meant redrawing the map of Europe to fit Wilson's idea of how Europeans should be governed.

Examples (*any three*):

1. Wilson created the country of Czechoslovakia by putting Czechs and Slavs together because they spoke the same language, although they had no other historical reason for being yoked.
2. Wilson created the country of Yugoslavia for Croatians, Serbians, Slovenes and Montenegrins, using common language as the only standard.
3. Wilson gave Austria's South Tyrol to Italy because Italians offered "proof" that this province was part of "historic Italy."
4. Hungarian land was given to Romania, making millions of Hungarians instant Romanians.
5. Millions of Germans were put into the newly recreated Poland.
6. Wilson considered, though he rejected, the possibility of uniting Austria and Germany on the basis of common language.

---

## Chapter 21: *VIVA CRISTO REY!* (Pages 127-132)

**Completion**

1. Students
2. embargo
3. Vera Cruz
4. Constitution
5. Eucharistic Adoration
6. Filippi
7. Religious
8. Flores
9. Cristeros
10. Moreno
11. Roberto
12. Valdez
13. sacrifice
14. Burke

**Multiple Choice**

| | | | |
|---|---|---|---|
| 1. | c | 6. | b |
| 2. | a | 7. | c |
| 3. | b | 8. | d |
| 4. | d | 9. | b |
| 5. | d | 10. | e |

**True/False**

| | | | |
|---|---|---|---|
| 1. | F | 8. | T |
| 2. | F | 9. | T |
| 3. | F | 10. | T |
| 4. | T | 11. | F |
| 5. | F | 12. | T |
| 6. | T | 13. | T |
| 7. | F | | |

**Matching**

| | | | |
|---|---|---|---|
| 1. | K | 8. | I |
| 2. | J | 9. | G |
| 3. | E | 10. | A |
| 4. | B | 11. | F |
| 5. | D | 12. | L |
| 6. | H | 13. | C |
| 7. | M | | |

**Mini-Essay Question**

On November 14, 1921, a man placed a time bomb hidden in a bouquet of flowers before the miraculous image of Our Lady of Guadalupe in the basilica. When the bomb exploded, many stained glass windows of the basilica shattered, and a heavy crucifix was twisted into a semicircle, but Juan Diego's tilma (with its miraculous image) and the glass in front of it was unharmed. The miracle served to strengthen the faith of the Mexicans, despite this attempt by the enemies of the Church to destroy their faith.

## Chapter 22: BOOM, DEPRESSION AND THE NEW DEAL (Pages 133-139)

**Completion**

1. isolationist
2. normalcy
3. alcoholic beverages/alcohol
4. permissiveness
5. Protestant
6. Ku Klux Klan
7. temple
8. Federal Reserve
9. boom
10. Coolidge
11. Hoover
12. Franklin Roosevelt
13. subsidiarity
14. Social Security

**Multiple Choice**

| | | | |
|---|---|---|---|
| 1. | b | 6. | a |
| 2. | c | 7. | e |
| 3. | e | 8. | b |
| 4. | e | 9. | d |
| 5. | c | 10. | b |

**True/False**

| | | | |
|---|---|---|---|
| 1. | F | 8. | T |
| 2. | T | 9. | F |
| 3. | F | 10. | F |
| 4. | T | 11. | T |
| 5. | F | 12. | T |
| 6. | F | 13. | T |
| 7. | T | | |

**Matching**

| | | | |
|---|---|---|---|
| 1. | H | 8. | B |
| 2. | M | 9. | D |
| 3. | F | 10. | I |
| 4. | A | 11. | C |
| 5. | E | 12. | J |
| 6. | K | 13. | G |
| 7. | L | | |

**Mini-Essay Question**

The Social Security Act seems like a perfect solution to the problem of helping people who cannot help themselves.

Problems (*any 3*):

1. Even very poor people had to have their wages reduced to pay into the fund.
2. Employers further reduce wages to compensate for payroll taxes.
3. Employers raise prices to cover the cost of payroll taxes.
4. Many families and communities do not take responsibility for providing for their elderly people.
5. Too many people rely too much on Social Security to take care of them in old age and therefore do not save.
6. More is paid out in benefits than was paid in, leading to increased Social Security tax on current workers.

---

## Chapter 23: THE UNITED STATES IN WORLD WAR II (Pages 141-146)

**Completion**

1. Poland
2. Great Britain
3. December 8, 1941
4. Bataan
5. Midway
6. Dwight D. Eisenhower
7. Sicily
8. strategic
9. Poland
10. Werner von Braun
11. Stauffenberg
12. Philippine
13. United Nations
14. Operation Keelhaul

**Multiple Choice**

| | | | |
|---|---|---|---|
| 1. | d | 6. | d |
| 2. | a | 7. | b |
| 3. | d | 8. | a |
| 4. | c | 9. | b |
| 5. | a | 10. | e |

**True/False**

| | | | |
|---|---|---|---|
| 1. | T | 8. | F |
| 2. | F | 9. | T |
| 3. | F | 10. | F |
| 4. | T | 11. | F |
| 5. | F | 12. | T |
| 6. | T | 13. | T |
| 7. | T | | |

**Matching**

| | | | |
|---|---|---|---|
| 1. | L | 8. | A |
| 2. | I | 9. | G |
| 3. | K | 10. | J |
| 4. | H | 11. | D |
| 5. | C | 12. | F |
| 6. | M | 13. | B |
| 7. | E | | |

**Mini-Essay Question**

The three leaders at the Yalta Conference—Roosevelt, Churchill and Stalin—agreed that all citizens of an Allied country that had been liberated by another Allied country would be returned to their homeland. Due to this secret agreement, even those, such as Vlasov's army and the Cossacks, who did not want to return to Communist Russia, were forced to go back. General Vlasov and his army were hanged or machine-gunned upon their return because they had rejected Communism. Whole families of Christian Cossacks were forced to return to live under Communist atheism. Both groups had appealed to the U.S. for help, but the U.S. ignored their pleas and forced them to go back.

Keelhauling was a punishment in some navies that involved tying a man with ropes, throwing him overboard and allowing him to be hauled under the ship's keel from side to side, usually causing death. Operation Keelhaul was the name given to the forced return of two million people at gunpoint because, for most of these people, to return to a Communist nation was like a death sentence.

## Chapter 24: THE BIRTH AND DEATH OF ANTI-COMMUNISM (Pages 147-153)

**Completion**

1. Berlin
2. Federal
3. Truman
4. Cold War
5. Marshall
6. Taiwan
7. insane
8. Rosenberg
9. Soviet
10. Pusan
11. Chinese
12. 38th
13. civil wars
14. Hungarian

**Multiple Choice**

| | | | |
|---|---|---|---|
| 1. | a | 6. | a |
| 2. | b | 7. | c |
| 3. | d | 8. | c |
| 4. | e | 9. | b |
| 5. | a | 10. | e |

**True/False**

| | | | |
|---|---|---|---|
| 1. | T | 8. | F |
| 2. | T | 9. | T |
| 3. | T | 10. | T |
| 4. | F | 11. | F |
| 5. | F | 12. | T |
| 6. | F | 13. | T |
| 7. | T | | |

**Matching**

| | | | |
|---|---|---|---|
| 1. | H | 8. | C |
| 2. | E | 9. | G |
| 3. | L | 10. | D |
| 4. | K | 11. | J |
| 5. | A | 12. | F |
| 6. | I | 13. | B |
| 7. | M | | |

**Mini-Essay Question**

Both of these men were attacked viciously, their reputations ruined and their personal lives damaged because other people did not believe the truth. Chambers became discouraged and pessimistic, while McCarthy became depressed and sought relief through alcohol. However, because of these two men, many Americans have come to better understand the evils of Communism.

---

## Chapter 25: COMMUNISTS VS. CHRISTIANS IN LATIN AMERICA (Pages 155-160)

**Completion**

1. Havana
2. July
3. Florida
4. Central
5. Berlin
6. submarines
7. Peronata
8. Renunciation
9. Lucan
10. Communists
11. Interior
12. sleep
13. pilgrimage
14. Cuba

**Multiple Choice**

| | | | |
|---|---|---|---|
| 1. | d | 6. | b |
| 2 | e | 7. | d |
| 3. | c | 8. | b |
| 4. | e | 9. | d |
| 5. | a | 10. | d |

**True/False**

| | | | |
|---|---|---|---|
| 1. | T | 8. | T |
| 2. | F | 9. | T |
| 3. | F | 10. | F |
| 4. | T | 11. | T |
| 5. | F | 12. | F |
| 6. | T | 13. | T |
| 7. | T | | |

**Matching**

| | | | |
|---|---|---|---|
| 1. | G | 8. | A |
| 2. | M | 9. | H |
| 3. | F | 10. | D |
| 4. | K | 11. | L |
| 5. | B | 12. | I |
| 6. | J | 13. | E |
| 7. | C | | |

**Mini-Essay Question**

The U.S. stopped supplying Batista with arms in 1958, making it much easier for the Communist Fidel Castro to take over. Then the U.S. helped train Cuban exiles to invade Cuba and overthrow Castro—but in 1961, on the very day that the Cuban exiles needed the U.S. the most, President Kennedy withdrew the order for U.S. planes to provide air coverage for them at the Bay of Pigs. The Cuban exiles were killed or taken prisoner by Communists. The failure of the invasion and the cruel repression following it broke the back of anti-Communist resistance in Cuba.

## Chapter 26: THE MORAL DECLINE OF AMERICA (Pages 161-167)

**Completion**

1. Earl Warren
2. neutrality
3. country
4. Diem
5. Thich Tri Quang
6. resistance
7. Tonkin
8. Revolution
9. Tet
10. Columbia
11. detente
12. Liberation
13. Texas
14. Afghanistan

**Multiple Choice**

| | | | |
|---|---|---|---|
| 1. | b | 6. | b |
| 2. | c | 7. | b |
| 3. | b | 8. | c |
| 4. | d | 9. | e |
| 5. | a | 10. | e |

**True/False**

| | | | |
|---|---|---|---|
| 1. | T | 8. | F |
| 2. | F | 9. | F |
| 3. | T | 10. | T |
| 4. | F | 11. | F |
| 5. | T | 12. | T |
| 6. | T | 13. | T |
| 7. | T | | |

**Matching**

| | | | |
|---|---|---|---|
| 1. | K | 8. | J |
| 2. | M | 9. | E |
| 3. | F | 10. | B |
| 4. | L | 11. | G |
| 5. | D | 12. | A |
| 6. | H | 13. | I |
| 7. | C | | |

**Mini-Essay Question**

*(Any five:)*

1. There has been a serious decline in religious and priestly vocations.
2. Almost all Catholic colleges and universities have become dominated by liberals, who deny doctrinal and moral absolutes and the authority of the Pope.
3. The feminist movement demands that women be "ordained."
4. Liberation theologians promote Marxism, and the Americanist Heresy is again finding an audience among Church leaders of the U.S.
5. Divorce with remarriage is common among Catholics.
6. "Annulments" are often granted by Church tribunals for any reason.
7. The encyclical *Humanae Vitae* (1968), which reaffirmed Catholic teaching that contraception is intrinsically immoral, was widely rejected by liberal intellectuals, by rank-and-file Catholics and by priests.
8. Bishops failed to take the disciplinary action needed to restore doctrinal and moral orthodoxy to the Catholic Church in America.